Amusing Ourselves
to Death

Amusing Ourselves to Death

Public Discourse in the Age of Show Business

Neil Postman

Elisabeth Sifton Books
Viking

ELISABETH SIFTON BOOKS · VIKING
Viking Penguin Inc., 40 West 23rd Street,
New York, New York 10010, U.S.A.
Penguin Books Ltd, Harmondsworth,
Middlesex, England
Penguin Books Australia Ltd, Ringwood,
Victoria, Australia
Penguin Books Canada Limited, 2801 John Street,
Markham, Ontario, Canada L3R 1B4
Penguin Books (N.Z.) Ltd, 182–190 Wairau Road,
Auckland 10, New Zealand

First published in 1985 by Viking Penguin Inc.
Published simultaneously in Canada

LIBRARY OF CONGRESS CATALOGING IN PUBLICATION DATA
Postman, Neil.
Amusing ourselves to death.
''Elisabeth Sifton books.''
Includes index.
1. Mass media—Influence.   I. Title.
P94.P63   1985   302.2'34   85-5335
ISBN 0-670-80454-1

Grateful acknowledgment is made to The New York Times Company for
permission to reprint from ''Combining TV, Books, Computers'' by Edward Fiske,
which appeared in the August 7, 1984, issue of The New York Times.
Copyright © 1984 by The New York Times Company.

Printed in the United States of America by
The Maple-Vail Book Manufacturing Group, Binghamton, New York
Set in Linotron Meridien
Designed by Ann Gold

Contents

Foreword

We were keeping our eye on 1984. When the year came and the prophecy didn't, thoughtful Americans sang softly in praise of themselves. The roots of liberal democracy had held. Wherever else the terror had happened, we, at least, had not been visited by Orwellian nightmares.

But we had forgotten that alongside Orwell's dark vision, there was another—slightly older, slightly less well known, equally chilling: Aldous Huxley's *Brave New World*. Contrary to common belief even among the educated, Huxley and Orwell did not prophesy the same thing. Orwell warns that we will be overcome by an externally imposed oppression. But in Huxley's vision, no Big Brother is required to deprive people of their autonomy, maturity and history. As he saw it, people will come to love their oppression, to adore the technologies that undo their capacities to think.

What Orwell feared were those who would ban books. What Huxley feared was that there would be no reason to ban a book, for there would be no one who wanted to read one. Orwell feared those who would deprive us of information. Huxley feared those who would give us so much that we would be reduced to passivity and egoism. Orwell feared that the truth would be concealed from us. Huxley feared the truth would be drowned in a sea of irrelevance. Orwell feared we would become a captive culture. Huxley feared we would become a trivial culture, preoccupied with some equivalent of the feelies, the orgy porgy, and the centrifugal bumblepuppy. As Huxley remarked in *Brave New World Revisited,* the civil libertarians and rationalists who are ever on the alert to oppose tyranny "failed to take into account man's almost infinite appetite for distractions." In *1984,* Huxley added, people are controlled by inflicting pain. In *Brave New World,* they are controlled by inflicting pleasure. In short, Orwell feared that what we hate will ruin us. Huxley feared that what we love will ruin us.

This book is about the possibility that Huxley, not Orwell, was right.

Part I.

I.

The Medium
Is the Metaphor

At different times in our history, different cities have been the focal point of a radiating American spirit. In the late eighteenth century, for example, Boston was the center of a political radicalism that ignited a shot heard round the world—a shot that could not have been fired any other place but the suburbs of Boston. At its report, all Americans, including Virginians, became Bostonians at heart. In the mid-nineteenth century, New York became the symbol of the idea of a melting-pot America—or at least a non-English one—as the wretched refuse from all over the world disembarked at Ellis Island and spread over the land their strange languages and even stranger ways. In the early twentieth century, Chicago, the city of big shoulders and heavy winds, came to symbolize the industrial energy and dynamism of America. If there is a statue of a hog butcher somewhere in Chicago, then it stands as a reminder of the time when America was railroads, cattle, steel mills and entrepreneurial adventures. If there is no such statue, there ought to be, just as there is a statue of a Minute Man to recall the Age of Boston, as the Statue of Liberty recalls the Age of New York.

Today, we must look to the city of Las Vegas, Nevada, as a metaphor of our national character and aspiration, its symbol a thirty-foot-high cardboard picture of a slot machine and a chorus girl. For Las Vegas is a city entirely devoted to the idea of entertainment, and as such proclaims the spirit of a culture in which all public discourse increasingly takes the form of entertainment. Our politics, religion, news, athletics, education and commerce have been transformed into congenial adjuncts of show business, largely without protest or even much popular notice. The result is that we are a people on the verge of amusing ourselves to death.

As I write, the President of the United States is a former Hollywood movie actor. One of his principal challengers in 1984 was once a featured player on television's most glamorous show of the 1960's, that is to say, an astronaut. Naturally, a movie has been made about his extraterrestrial adventure. Former nominee George McGovern has hosted the popular television show "Saturday Night Live." So has a candidate of more recent vintage, the Reverend Jesse Jackson.

Meanwhile, former President Richard Nixon, who once claimed he lost an election because he was sabotaged by makeup men, has offered Senator Edward Kennedy advice on how to make a serious run for the presidency: lose twenty pounds. Although the Constitution makes no mention of it, it would appear that fat people are now effectively excluded from running for high political office. Probably bald people as well. Almost certainly those whose looks are not significantly enhanced by the cosmetician's art. Indeed, we may have reached the point where cosmetics has replaced ideology as the field of expertise over which a politician must have competent control.

America's journalists, i.e., television newscasters, have not missed the point. Most spend more time with their hair dryers than with their scripts, with the result that they comprise the most glamorous group of people this side of Las Vegas. Although the Federal Communications Act makes no mention of it, those without camera appeal are excluded from addressing the public about what is called "the news of the day." Those with camera appeal can command salaries exceeding one million dollars a year.

American businessmen discovered, long before the rest of us, that the quality and usefulness of their goods are subordinate to the artifice of their display; that, in fact, half the principles of

capitalism as praised by Adam Smith or condemned by Karl
Marx are irrelevant. Even the Japanese, who are said to make
better cars than the Americans, know that economics is less a
science than a performing art, as Toyota's yearly advertising
budget confirms.

Not long ago, I saw Billy Graham join with Shecky Green,
Red Buttons; Dionne Warwick, Milton Berle and other theolo-
gians in a tribute to George Burns, who was celebrating himself
for surviving eighty years in show business. The Reverend
Graham exchanged one-liners with Burns about making prepa-
rations for Eternity. Although the Bible makes no mention of it,
the Reverend Graham assured the audience that God loves
those who make people laugh. It was an honest mistake. He
merely mistook NBC for God.

Dr. Ruth Westheimer is a psychologist who has a popular radio program and a nightclub act in which she informs her audiences about sex in all of its infinite variety and in language once
reserved for the bedroom and street corners. She is almost as
entertaining as the Reverend Billy Graham, and has been
quoted as saying, "I don't start out to be funny. But if it comes
out that way, I use it. If they call me an entertainer, I say that's
great. When a professor teaches with a sense of humor, people
walk away remembering." [1] She did not say what they remember or of what use their remembering is. But she has a point: It's
great to be an entertainer. Indeed, in America God favors all
those who possess both a talent and a format to amuse, whether
they be preachers, athletes, entrepreneurs, politicians, teachers
or journalists. In America, the least amusing people are its professional entertainers.

Culture watchers and worriers—those of the type who read
books like this one—will know that the examples above are not
aberrations but, in fact, clichés. There is no shortage of critics
who have observed and recorded the dissolution of public discourse in America and its conversion into the arts of show business. But most of them, I believe, have barely begun to tell the

story of the origin and meaning of this descent into a vast triviality. Those who have written vigorously on the matter tell us, for example, that what is happening is the residue of an exhausted capitalism; or, on the contrary, that it is the tasteless fruit of the maturing of capitalism; or that it is the neurotic aftermath of the Age of Freud; or the retribution of our allowing God to perish; or that it all comes from the old stand-bys, greed and ambition.

I have attended carefully to these explanations, and I do not say there is nothing to learn from them. Marxists, Freudians, Lévi-Straussians, even Creation Scientists are not to be taken lightly. And, in any case, I should be very surprised if the story I have to tell is anywhere near the whole truth. We are all, as Huxley says someplace, Great Abbreviators, meaning that none of us has the wit to know the whole truth, the time to tell it if we believed we did, or an audience so gullible as to accept it. But you *will* find an argument here that presumes a clearer grasp of the matter than many that have come before. Its value, such as it is, resides in the directness of its perspective, which has its origins in observations made 2,300 years ago by Plato. It is an argument that fixes its attention on the forms of human conversation, and postulates that how we are obliged to conduct such conversations will have the strongest possible influence on what ideas we can conveniently express. And what ideas are convenient to express inevitably become the important content of a culture.

I use the word "conservation" metaphorically to refer not only to speech but to all techniques and technologies that permit people of a particular culture to exchange messages. In this sense, all culture is a conversation or, more precisely, a corporation of conversations, conducted in a variety of symbolic modes. Our attention here is on how forms of public discourse regulate and even dictate what kind of content can issue from such forms.

To take a simple example of what this means, consider the

primitive technology of smoke signals. While I do not know exactly what content was once carried in the smoke signals of American Indians, I can safely guess that it did not include philosophical argument. Puffs of smoke are insufficiently complex to express ideas on the nature of existence, and even if they were not, a Cherokee philosopher would run short of either wood or blankets long before he reached his second axiom. You cannot use smoke to do philosophy. Its form excludes the content.

To take an example closer to home: As I suggested earlier, it is implausible to imagine that anyone like our twenty-seventh President, the multi-chinned, three-hundred-pound William Howard Taft, could be put forward as a presidential candidate in today's world. The shape of a man's body is largely irrelevant to the shape of his ideas when he is addressing a public in writing or on the radio or, for that matter, in smoke signals. But it is quite relevant on television. The grossness of a three-hundred-pound image, even a talking one, would easily overwhelm any logical or spiritual subtleties conveyed by speech. For on television, discourse is conducted largely through visual imagery, which is to say that television gives us a conversation in images, not words. The emergence of the image-manager in the political arena and the concomitant decline of the speech writer attest to the fact that television demands a different kind of content from other media. You cannot do political philosophy on television. Its form works against the content.

To give still another example, one of more complexity: The information, the content, or, if you will, the "stuff" that makes up what is called "the news of the day" did not exist—could not exist—in a world that lacked the media to give it expression. I do not mean that things like fires, wars, murders and love affairs did not, ever and always, happen in places all over the world. I mean that lacking a technology to advertise them, people could not attend to them, could not include them in their daily business. Such information simply could not exist as part of the content of culture. This idea—that there is a content called "the news of the day"—was entirely created by the telegraph (and since amplified by newer media), which made it possible to move decontextualized information over vast spaces at incredible speed. The news of the day is a figment of our technological imagination. It is, quite precisely, a media event. We attend to fragments of events from all over the world because we have multiple media whose forms are well suited to fragmented conversation. Cultures without speed-of-light media—let us say, cultures in which smoke signals are the most efficient space-conquering tool available—do not have news of the day. Without a medium to create its form, the news of the day does not exist.

To say it, then, as plainly as I can, this book is an inquiry into and a lamentation about the most significant American cultural fact of the second half of the twentieth century: the decline of the Age of Typography and the ascendancy of the Age of Television. This change-over has dramatically and irreversibly shifted the content and meaning of public discourse, since two media so vastly different cannot accommodate the same ideas. As the influence of print wanes, the content of politics, religion, education, and anything else that comprises public business must change and be recast in terms that are most suitable to television.

If all of this sounds suspiciously like Marshall McLuhan's aphorism, the medium is the message, I will not disavow the association (although it is fashionable to do so among respectable scholars who, were it not for McLuhan, would today be mute). I met McLuhan thirty years ago when I was a graduate student and he an unknown English professor. I believed then, as I believe now, that he spoke in the tradition of Orwell and Huxley—that is, as a prophesier, and I have remained steadfast to his teaching that the clearest way to see through a culture is to attend to its tools for conversation. I might add that my interest in this point of view was first stirred by a prophet far more

formidable than McLuhan, more ancient than Plato. In studying the Bible as a young man, I found intimations of the idea
that forms of media favor particular kinds of content and therefore are capable of taking command of a culture. I refer specifically to the Decalogue, the Second Commandment of which
prohibits the Israelites from making concrete images of anything. "Thou shalt not make unto thee any graven image, any
likeness of any thing that is in heaven above, or that is in the
earth beneath, or that is in the water beneath the earth." I wondered then, as so many others have, as to why the God of these
people would have included instructions on how they were to
symbolize, or not symbolize, their experience. It is a strange
injunction to include as part of an ethical system *unless its author
assumed a connection between forms of human communication and
the quality of a culture.* We may hazard a guess that a people who
are being asked to embrace an abstract, universal deity would
be rendered unfit to do so by the habit of drawing pictures or
making statues or depicting their ideas in any concrete, icono-
graphic forms. The God of the Jews was to exist in the Word
and through the Word, an unprecedented conception requiring
the highest order of abstract thinking. Iconography thus became
blasphemy so that a new kind of God could enter a culture.
People like ourselves who are in the process of converting their
culture from word-centered to image-centered might profit by
reflecting on this Mosaic injunction. But even if I am wrong in
these conjectures, it is, I believe, a wise and particularly relevant
supposition that the media of communication available to a culture are a dominant influence on the formation of the culture's
intellectual and social preoccupations.

Speech, of course, is the primal and indispensable medium. It
made us human, keeps us human, and in fact defines what human means. This is not to say that if there were no other means
of communication all humans would find it equally convenient
to speak about the same things in the same way. We know
enough about language to understand that variations in the

structures of languages will result in variations in what may be called "world view." How people think about time and space, and about things and processes, will be greatly influenced by the grammatical features of their language. We dare not suppose therefore that all human minds are unanimous in understanding how the world is put together. But how much more divergence there is in world view among different cultures can be imagined when we consider the great number and variety of tools for conversation that go beyond speech. For although culture is a creation of speech, it is recreated anew by every medium of communication—from painting to hieroglyphs to the alphabet to television. Each medium, like language itself, makes possible a unique mode of discourse by providing a new orientation for thought, for expression, for sensibility. Which, of course, is what McLuhan meant in saying the medium is the message. His aphorism, however, is in need of amendment because, as it stands, it may lead one to confuse a message with a metaphor. A message denotes a specific, concrete statement about the world. But the forms of our media, including the symbols through which they permit conversation, do not make such statements. They are rather like metaphors, working by unobtrusive but powerful implication to enforce their special definitions of reality. Whether we are experiencing the world through the lens of speech or the printed word or the television camera, our media-metaphors classify the world for us, sequence it, frame it, enlarge it, reduce it, color it, argue a case for what the world is like. As Ernst Cassirer remarked:

> Physical reality seems to recede in proportion as man's symbolic activity advances. Instead of dealing with the things themselves man is in a sense constantly conversing with himself. He has so enveloped himself in linguistic forms, in artistic images, in mythical symbols or religious rites that he cannot see or know anything except by the interposition of [an] artificial medium.[2]

'What is peculiar about such interpositions of media is that their role in directing what we will see or know is so rarely noticed. A person who reads a book or who watches television or who glances at his watch is not usually interested in how his mind is organized and controlled by these events, still less in what idea of the world is suggested by a book, television, or a watch. But there are men and women who have noticed these things, especially in our own times. Lewis Mumford, for example, has been one of our great noticers. He is not the sort of a man who looks at a clock merely to see what time it is. Not that he lacks interest in the content of clocks, which is of concern to everyone from moment to moment, but he is far more interested in how a clock creates the idea of "moment to moment." He attends to the philosophy of clocks, to clocks as metaphor, about which our education has had little to say and clock makers nothing at all. "The clock," Mumford has concluded, "is a piece of power machinery whose 'product' is seconds and minutes." In manufacturing such a product, the clock has the effect of disassociating time from human events and thus nourishes the belief ·in an independent world of mathematically measurable sequences. Moment to moment, it turns out, is not God's conception, or nature's. It is man conversing with himself about and through a piece of machinery he created.

In Mumford's great book *Technics and Civilization*, he shows how, beginning in the fourteenth century, the clock made us into time-keepers, and then time-savers, and now time-servers. In the process, we have learned irreverence toward the sun and the seasons, for in a world made up of seconds and minutes, the authority of nature is superseded. Indeed, as Mumford points out, with the invention of the clock, Eternity ceased to serve as the measure and focus of human events. And thus, though few would have imagined the connection, the inexorable ticking of the clock may have had more to do with the weakening of God's supremacy than all the treatises produced by the philosophers of the Enlightenment; that is to say, the clock introduced a new form of conversation between man and God, in which God appears to have been the loser. Perhaps Moses should have included another Commandment: Thou shalt not make mechanical representations of time.

That the alphabet introduced a new form of conversation between man and man is by now a commonplace among scholars. To be able to *see* one's utterances rather than only to hear them is no small matter, though our education, once again, has had little to say about this. Nonetheless, it is clear that phonetic writing created a new conception of knowledge, as well as a new sense of intelligence, of audience and of posterity, all of which Plato recognized at an early stage in the development of texts. "No man of intelligence," he wrote in his Seventh Letter, "will venture to express his philosophical views in language, especially not in language that is unchangeable, which is true of that which is set down in written characters." This notwithstanding, he wrote voluminously and understood better than anyone else that the setting down of views in written characters would be the beginning of philosophy, not its end. Philosophy cannot exist without criticism, and writing makes it possible and convenient to subject thought to a continuous and concentrated scrutiny. Writing freezes speech and in so doing gives birth to the grammarian, the logician, the rhetorician, the historian, the scientist—all those who must hold language before them so that they can see what it means, where it errs, and where it is leading.

Plato knew all of this, which means that he knew that writing would bring about a perceptual revolution: a shift from the ear to the eye as an organ of language processing. Indeed, there is a legend that to encourage such a shift Plato insisted that his students study geometry before entering his Academy. If true, it was a sound idea, for as the great literary critic Northrop Frye has remarked, "the written word is far more powerful than simply a reminder: it re-creates the past in the present, and gives us, not the familiar remembered thing, but the glittering intensity of the summoned-up hallucination."[3]

All that Plato surmised about the consequences of writing is now well understood by anthropologists, especially those who have studied cultures in which speech is the only source of complex conversation. Anthropologists know that the written word, as Northrop Frye meant to suggest, is not merely an echo of a speaking voice. It is another kind of voice altogether, a conjurer's trick of the first order. It must certainly have appeared that way to those who invented it, and that is why we should not be surprised that the Egyptian god Thoth, who is alleged to have brought writing to the King Thamus, was also the god of magic. People like ourselves may see nothing wondrous in writing, but our anthropologists know how strange and magical it appears to a purely oral people—a conversation with no one and yet with everyone. What could be stranger than the silence one encounters when addressing a question to a text? What could be more metaphysically puzzling than addressing an unseen audience, as every writer of books must do? And correcting oneself because one knows that an unknown reader will disapprove or misunderstand?

I bring all of this up because what my book is about is how our own tribe is undergoing a vast and trembling shift from the magic of writing to the magic of electronics. What I mean to point out here is that the introduction into a culture of a technique such as writing or a clock is not merely an extension of man's power to bind time but a transformation of his way of thinking—and, of course, of the content of his culture. And that is what I mean to say by calling a medium a metaphor. We are told in school, quite correctly, that a metaphor suggests what a thing is like by comparing it to something else. And by the power of its suggestion, it so fixes a conception in our minds that we cannot imagine the one thing without the other: Light is a wave; language, a tree; God, a wise and venerable man; the mind, a dark cavern illuminated by knowledge. And if these metaphors no longer serve us, we must, in the nature of the matter, find others that will. Light is a particle; language, a river; God (as Bertrand Russell proclaimed), a differential equation; the mind, a garden that yearns to be cultivated.

But our media-metaphors are not so explicit or so vivid as these, and they are far more complex. In understanding their metaphorical function, we must take into account the symbolic forms of their information, the source of their information, the quantity and speed of their information, the context in which their information is experienced. Thus, it takes some digging to get at them, to grasp, for example, that a clock recreates time as an independent, mathematically precise sequence; that writing recreates the mind as a tablet on which experience is written; that the telegraph recreates news as a commodity. And yet, such digging becomes easier if we start from the assumption that in every tool we create, an idea is embedded that goes beyond the function of the thing itself. It has been pointed out, for example, that the invention of eyeglasses in the twelfth century not only made it possible to improve defective vision but suggested the idea that human beings need not accept as final either the endowments of nature or the ravages of time. Eyeglasses refuted the belief that anatomy is destiny by putting forward the idea that our bodies as well as our minds are improvable. I do not think it goes too far to say that there is a link between the invention of eyeglasses in the twelfth century and gene-splitting research in the twentieth.

Even such an instrument as the microscope, hardly a tool of everyday use, had embedded within it a quite astonishing idea, not about biology but about psychology. By revealing a world hitherto hidden from view, the microscope suggested a possibility about the structure of the mind.

If things are not what they seem, if microbes lurk, unseen, on and under our skin, if the invisible controls the visible, then is it not possible that ids and egos and superegos also lurk somewhere unseen? What else is psychoanalysis but a microscope of the mind? Where do our notions of mind come from if not from metaphors generated by our tools? What does it mean to say that someone has an IQ of 126? There are no numbers in people's heads. Intelligence does not have quantity or magnitude, except as we believe that it does. And why do we believe that it does? Because we have tools that imply that this is what the mind is like. Indeed, our tools for thought suggest to us what our bodies are like, as when someone refers to her "biological clock," or when we talk of our "genetic codes," or when we read someone's face like a book, or when our facial expressions telegraph our intentions.

When Galileo remarked that the language of nature is written in mathematics, he meant it only as a metaphor. Nature itself does not speak. Neither do our minds or our bodies or, more to the point of this book, our bodies politic. Our conversations about nature and about ourselves are conducted in whatever "languages" we find it possible and convenient to employ. We do not see nature or intelligence or human motivation or ideology as "it" is but only as our languages are. And our languages are our media. Our media are our metaphors. Our metaphors create the content of our culture.

2.

Media as Epistemology

It is my intention in this book to show that a great media-metaphor shift has taken place in America, with the result that the content of much of our public discourse has become dangerous nonsense. With this in view, my task in the chapters ahead is straightforward. I must, first, demonstrate how, under the governance of the printing press, discourse in America was different from what it is now—generally coherent, serious and rational; and then how, under the governance of television, it has become shriveled and absurd. But to avoid the possibility that my analysis will be interpreted as standard-brand academic whimpering, a kind of elitist complaint against "junk" on television, I must first explain that my focus is on epistemology, not on aesthetics or literary criticism. Indeed, I appreciate junk as much as the next fellow, and I know full well that the printing press has generated enough of it to fill the Grand Canyon to overflowing. Television is not old enough to have matched printing's output of junk.

And so, I raise no objection to television's junk. The best things on television _are_ its junk, and no one and nothing is seriously threatened by it. Besides, we do not measure a culture by its output of undisguised trivialities but by what it claims as significant. Therein is our problem, for television is at its most trivial and, therefore, most dangerous when its aspirations are high, when it presents itself as a carrier of important cultural conversations. The irony here is that this is what intellectuals and critics are constantly urging television to do. The trouble with such people is that they do not take television seriously enough. For, like the printing press, television is nothing less than a philosophy of rhetoric. To talk seriously about television, one must therefore talk of epistemology. All other commentary is in itself trivial.

Epistemology is a complex and usually opaque subject concerned with the origins and nature of knowledge. The part of its subject matter that is relevant here is the interest it takes in definitions of truth and the sources from which such definitions come. In particular, I want to show that definitions of truth are derived, at least in part, from the character of the media of communication through which information is conveyed. I want to discuss how media are implicated in our epistemologies.

In the hope of simplifying what I mean by the title of this chapter, media as epistemology, I find it helpful to borrow a word from Northrop Frye, who has made use of a principle he calls *resonance*. "Through resonance," he writes, "a particular statement in a particular context acquires a universal significance."[1] Frye offers as an opening example the phrase "the grapes of wrath," which first appears in Isaiah in the context of a celebration of a prospective massacre of Edomites. But the phrase, Frye continues, "has long ago flown away from this context into many new contexts, contexts that give dignity to the human situation instead of merely reflecting its bigotries."[2] Having said this, Frye extends the idea of resonance so that it goes beyond phrases and sentences. A character in a play or story—Hamlet, for example, or Lewis Carroll's Alice—may have resonance. Objects may have resonance, and so may countries: "The smallest details of the geography of two tiny chopped-up countries, Greece and Israel, have imposed themselves on our consciousness until they have become part of the map of our own imaginative world, whether we have ever seen these countries or not."[3]

In addressing the question of the source of resonance, Frye concludes that metaphor is the generative force—that is, the power of a phrase, a book, a character, or a history to unify and invest with meaning a variety of attitudes or experiences. Thus, Athens becomes a metaphor of intellectual excellence, wherever we find it; Hamlet, a metaphor of brooding indecisiveness; Alice's wanderings, a metaphor of a search for order in a world of semantic nonsense.

I now depart from Frye (who, I am certain, would raise no objection) but I take his word along with me. Every medium of communication, I am claiming, has resonance, for resonance is metaphor writ large. Whatever the original and limited context of its use may have been, a medium has the power to fly far beyond that context into new and unexpected ones. Because of the way it directs us to organize our minds and integrate our experience of the world, it imposes itself on our consciousness and social institutions in myriad forms. It sometimes has the power to become implicated in our concepts of piety, or goodness, or beauty. And it is always implicated in the ways we define and regulate our ideas of truth.

To explain how this happens—how the bias of a medium sits heavy, felt but unseen, over a culture—I offer three cases of truth-telling.

The first is drawn from a tribe in western Africa that has no writing system but whose rich oral tradition has given form to its ideas of civil law.[4] When a dispute arises, the complainants come before the chief of the tribe and state their grievances. With no written law to guide him, the task of the chief is to search through his vast repertoire of proverbs and sayings to find one that suits the situation and is equally satisfying to both complainants. That accomplished, all parties are agreed that justice has been done, that the truth has been served. You will recognize, of course, that this was largely the method of Jesus and other Biblical figures who, living in an essentially oral culture, drew upon all of the resources of speech, including mnemonic devices, formulaic expressions and parables, as a means of discovering and revealing truth. As Walter Ong points out, in oral cultures proverbs and sayings are not occasional devices: "They are incessant. They form the substance of thought itself. Thought in any extended form is impossible without them, for it consists in them."[5]

To people like ourselves any reliance on proverbs and sayings is reserved largely for resolving disputes among or with children. "Possession is nine-tenths of the law." "First come, first served." "Haste makes waste." These are forms of speech we pull out in small crises with our young but would think ridiculous to produce in a courtroom where "serious" matters are to be decided. Can you imagine a bailiff asking a jury if it has reached a decision and receiving the reply that "to err is human but to forgive is divine"? Or even better, "Let us render unto Caesar that which is Caesar's and to God that which is God's"? For the briefest moment, the judge might be charmed but if a "serious" language form is not immediately forthcoming, the jury may end up with a longer sentence than most guilty defendants.

Judges, lawyers and defendants do not regard proverbs or sayings as a relevant response to legal disputes. In this, they are separated from the tribal chief by a media-metaphor. For in a print-based courtroom, where law books, briefs, citations and other written materials define and organize the method of finding the truth, the oral tradition has lost much of its resonance— but not all of it. Testimony is expected to be given orally, on the assumption that the spoken, not the written, word is a truer reflection of the state of mind of a witness. Indeed, in many courtrooms jurors are not permitted to take notes, nor are they given written copies of the judge's explanation of the law. Jurors are expected to *hear* the truth, or its opposite, not to read it. Thus, we may say that there is a clash of resonances in our concept of legal truth. On the one hand, there is a residual belief in the power of speech, and speech alone, to carry the truth; on the other hand, there is a much stronger belief in the authenticity of writing and, in particular, printing. This second belief has little tolerance for poetry, proverbs, sayings, parables or any other expressions of oral wisdom. The law is what legislators and judges have written. In our culture, lawyers do not have to be wise; they need to be well briefed.

A similar paradox exists in universities, and with roughly the same distribution of resonances; that is to say, there are a few residual traditions based on the notion that speech is the primary carrier of truth. But for the most part, university conceptions of truth are tightly bound to the structure and logic of the printed word. To exemplify this point, I draw here on a personal experience that occurred during a still widely practiced medieval ritual known as a "doctoral oral." I use the word *medieval* literally, for in the Middle Ages students were always examined orally, and the tradition is carried forward in the assumption that a candidate must be able to talk competently about his written work. But, of course, the written work matters most.

In the case I have in mind, the issue of what is a legitimate form of truth-telling was raised to a level of consciousness rarely achieved. The candidate had included in his thesis a footnote, intended as documentation of a quotation, which read: "Told to the investigator at the Roosevelt Hotel on January 18, 1981, in the presence of Arthur Lingeman and Jerrold Gross." This citation drew the attention of no fewer than four of the five oral examiners, all of whom observed that it was hardly suitable as a form of documentation and that it ought to be replaced by a citation from a book or article. "You are not a journalist," one professor remarked. "You are supposed to be a scholar." Perhaps because the candidate knew of no published statement of what he was told at the Roosevelt Hotel, he defended himself vigorously on the grounds that there were witnesses to what he was told, that they were available to attest to the accuracy of the quotation, and that the form in which an idea is conveyed is irrelevant to its truth. Carried away on the wings of his eloquence, the candidate argued further that there were more than three hundred references to published works in his thesis and that it was extremely unlikely that any of them would be checked for accuracy by the examiners, by which he meant to raise the question, Why do you *assume* the accuracy of a print-referenced citation but not a speech-referenced one?

The answer he received took the following line: You are mistaken in believing that the form in which an idea is conveyed is irrelevant to its truth. In the academic world, the published word is invested with greater prestige and authenticity than the spoken word. What people say is assumed to be more casually uttered than what they write. The written word is assumed to have been reflected upon and revised by its author, reviewed by authorities and editors. It is easier to verify or refute, and it is invested with an impersonal and objective character, which is why, no doubt, you have referred to yourself in your thesis as "the investigator" and not by your name; that is to say, the written word is, by its nature, addressed to the world, not an individual. The written word endures, the spoken word disappears; and that is why writing is closer to the truth than speaking. Moreover, we are sure you would prefer that this commission produce a written statement that you have passed your examination (should you do so) than for us merely to tell you that you have, and leave it at that. Our written statement would represent the "truth." Our oral agreement would be only a rumor.

The candidate wisely said no more on the matter except to indicate that he would make whatever changes the commission suggested and that he profoundly wished that should he pass the "oral," a written document would attest to that fact. He did pass, and in time the proper words were written.

A third example of the influence of media on our epistemologies can be drawn from the trial of the great Socrates. At the opening of Socrates' defense, addressing a jury of five hundred, he apologizes for not having a well-prepared speech. He tells his Athenian brothers that he will falter, begs that they not interrupt him on that account, asks that they regard him as they would a stranger from another city, and promises that he will tell them the truth, without adornment or eloquence. Beginning this way was, of course, characteristic of Socrates, but it was not characteristic of the age in which he lived. For, as Socrates knew full well, his Athenian brothers did not regard the principles of rhetoric and the expression of truth to be independent of each other. People like ourselves find great appeal in Socrates' plea because we are accustomed to thinking of rhetoric as an ornament of speech—most often pretentious, superficial and unnecessary. But to the people who invented it, the Sophists of fifth-century B.C. Greece and their heirs, rhetoric was not merely an opportunity for dramatic performance but a near indispensable means of organizing evidence and proofs, and therefore of communicating truth.[6]

It was not only a key element in the education of Athenians (far more important than philosophy) but a preeminent art form. To the Greeks, rhetoric was a form of spoken writing. Though it always implied oral performance, its power to reveal the truth resided in the written word's power to display arguments in orderly progression. Although Plato himself disputed this conception of truth (as we might guess from Socrates' plea), his contemporaries believed that rhetoric was the proper means through which "right opinion" was to be both discovered and articulated. To disdain rhetorical rules, to speak one's thoughts in a random manner, without proper emphasis or appropriate passion, was considered demeaning to the audience's intelligence and suggestive of falsehood. Thus, we can assume that many of the 280 jurors who cast a guilty ballot against Socrates did so because his manner was not consistent with truthful matter, as they understood the connection.

The point I am leading to by this and the previous examples is that the concept of truth is intimately linked to the biases of forms of expression. Truth does not, and never has, come unadorned. It must appear in its proper clothing or it is not acknowledged, which is a way of saying that the "truth" is a kind of cultural prejudice. Each culture conceives of it as being most authentically expressed in certain symbolic forms that another culture may regard as trivial or irrelevant. Indeed, to the Greeks of Aristotle's time, and for two thousand years afterward, scientific truth was best discovered and expressed by deducing the nature of things from a set of self-evident premises, which accounts for Aristotle's believing that women have fewer teeth than men, and that babies are healthier if conceived when the wind is in the north. Aristotle was twice married but so far as we know, it did not occur to him to ask either of his wives if he could count her teeth. And as for his obstetric opinions, we are safe in assuming he used no questionnaires and hid behind no curtains. Such acts would have seemed to him both vulgar and unnecessary, for that was not the way to ascertain the truth of things. The language of deductive logic provided a surer road.

We must not be too hasty in mocking Aristotle's prejudices. We have enough of our own, as for example, the equation we moderns make of truth and quantification. In this prejudice, we come astonishingly close to the mystical beliefs of Pythagoras and his followers who attempted to submit all of life to the sovereignty of numbers. Many of our psychologists, sociologists, economists and other latter-day cabalists will have numbers to tell them the truth or they will have nothing. Can you imagine, for example, a modern economist articulating truths about our standard of living by reciting a poem? Or by telling what happened to him during a late-night walk through East St. Louis? Or by offering a series of proverbs and parables, beginning with the saying about a rich man, a camel, and the eye of a needle? The first would be regarded as irrelevant, the second merely anecdotal, the last childish. Yet these forms of language are certainly capable of expressing truths about economic relationships, as well as any other relationships, and indeed have been employed by various peoples. But to the modern mind, resonating with different media-metaphors, the truth in economics is believed to be best discovered and expressed in numbers. Perhaps it is. I will not argue the point. I mean only to call attention to the fact that there is a certain measure of arbitrariness in the forms that truth-telling may take. We must remember that Galileo merely said that the language of *nature* is written in mathematics. He did not say *everything* is. And even the truth about nature need not be expressed in mathematics. For most of human history, the language of nature has been the language of myth and ritual. These forms, one might add, had the virtues of leaving nature unthreatened and of encouraging the belief that human beings are part of it. It hardly befits a people who stand ready to blow up the planet to praise themselves too vigorously for having found the true way to talk about nature.

In saying this, I am not making a case for epistemological relativism. Some ways of truth-telling are better than others, and therefore have a healthier influence on the cultures that adopt them. Indeed, I hope to persuade you that the decline of a print-based epistemology and the accompanying rise of a television-based epistemology has had grave consequences for public life, that we are getting sillier by the minute. And that is why it is necessary for me to drive hard the point that the weight assigned to any form of truth-telling is a function of the influence of media of communication. "Seeing is believing" has always had a preeminent status as an epistemological axiom, but "saying is believing," "reading is believing," "counting is believing," "deducing is believing," and "feeling is believing" are others that have risen or fallen in importance as cultures have undergone media change. As a culture moves from orality to writing to printing to televising, its ideas of truth move with it. Every philosophy is the philosophy of a stage of life, Nietzsche remarked. To which we might add that every epistemology is the epistemology of a stage of media development. Truth, like time itself, is a product of a conversation man has with himself about and through the techniques of communication he has invented.

Since intelligence is primarily defined as one's capacity to grasp the truth of things, it follows that what a culture means by intelligence is derived from the character of its important forms of communication. In a purely oral culture, intelligence is often associated with aphoristic ingenuity, that is, the power to invent compact sayings of wide applicability. The wise Solomon, we are told in First Kings, knew three thousand proverbs. In a print culture, people with such a talent are thought to be quaint at best, more likely pompous bores. In a purely oral culture, a high value is always placed on the power to memorize, for where there are no written words, the human mind must function as a mobile library. To forget how something is to be said or done is a danger to the community and a gross form of stupidity. In a print culture, the memorization of a poem, a menu, a law or most anything else is merely charming. It is almost always functionally irrelevant and certainly not considered a sign of high intelligence.

Although the general character of print-intelligence would be known to anyone who would be reading this book, you may arrive at a reasonably detailed definition of it by simply considering what is demanded of you *as you read this book.* You are required, first of all, to remain more or less immobile for a fairly long time. If you cannot do this (with this or any other book), our culture may label you as anything from hyperkinetic to undisciplined; in any case, as suffering from some sort of intellectual deficiency. The printing press makes rather stringent demands on our bodies as well as our minds. Controlling your body is, however, only a minimal requirement. You must also have learned to pay no attention to the shapes of the letters on the page. You must see through them, so to speak, so that you can go directly to the meanings of the words they form. If you are preoccupied with the shapes of the letters, you will be an intolerably inefficient reader, likely to be thought stupid. If you have learned how to get to meanings without aesthetic distraction, you are required to assume an attitude of detachment and objectivity. This includes your bringing to the task what

Bertrand Russell called an "immunity to eloquence," meaning that you are able to distinguish between the sensuous pleasure, or charm, or ingratiating tone (if such there be) of the words, and the logic of their argument. But at the same time, you must be able to tell from the tone of the language what is the author's attitude toward the subject and toward the reader. You must, in other words, know the difference between a joke and an argument. And in judging the quality of an argument, you must be able to do several things at once, including delaying a verdict until the entire argument is finished, holding in mind questions until you have determined where, when or if the text answers them, and bringing to bear on the text all of your relevant experience as a counterargument to what is being proposed. You must also be able to withhold those parts of your knowledge and experience which, in fact, do not have a bearing on the argument. And in preparing yourself to do all of this, you must have divested yourself of the belief that words are magical and, above all, have learned to negotiate the world of abstractions, for there are very few phrases and sentences in this book that require you to call forth concrete images. In a print-culture, we are apt to say of people who are not intelligent that we must "draw them pictures" so that they may understand. Intelligence implies that one can dwell comfortably without pictures, in a field of concepts and generalizations.

To be able to do all of these things, and more, constitutes a primary definition of intelligence in a culture whose notions of truth are organized around the printed word. In the next two chapters I want to show that in the eighteenth and nineteenth centuries, America was such a place, perhaps the most print-oriented culture ever to have existed. In subsequent chapters, I want to show that in the twentieth century, our notions of truth and our ideas of intelligence have changed as a result of new media displacing the old.

But I do not wish to oversimplify the matter more than is necessary. In particular, I want to conclude by making three points that may serve as a defense against certain counterarguments that careful readers may have already formed.

The first is that at no point do I care to claim that changes in media bring about changes in the structure of people's minds or changes in their cognitive capacities. There are some who make this claim, or come close to it (for example, Jerome Bruner, Jack Goody, Walter Ong, Marshall McLuhan, Julian Jaynes, and Eric Havelock).[7] I am inclined to think they are right, but my argument does not require it. Therefore, I will not burden myself with arguing the possibility, for example, that oral people are less developed intellectually, in some Piagetian sense, than writing people, or that "television" people are less developed intellectually than either. My argument is limited to saying that a major new medium changes the structure of discourse; it does so by encouraging certain uses of the intellect, by favoring certain definitions of intelligence and wisdom, and by demanding a certain kind of content—in a phrase, by creating new forms of truth-telling. I will say once again that I am no relativist in this matter, and that I believe the epistemology created by television not only is inferior to a print-based epistemology but is dangerous and absurdist.

The second point is that the epistemological shift I have intimated, and will describe in detail, has not yet included (and perhaps never will include) everyone and everything. While some old media do, in fact, disappear (e.g., pictographic writing and illuminated manuscripts) and with them, the institutions and cognitive habits they favored, other forms of conversation will always remain. Speech, for example, and writing. Thus the epistemology of new forms such as television does not have an entirely unchallenged influence.

I find it useful to think of the situation in this way: Changes in the symbolic environment are like changes in the natural environment; they are both gradual and additive at first, and then, all at once, a critical mass is achieved, as the physicists say. A river that has slowly been polluted suddenly becomes toxic; most of the fish perish; swimming becomes a danger to health. But even then, the river may look the same and one may still take a boat ride on it. In other words, even when life has been taken from it, the river does not disappear, nor do all of its uses, but its value has been seriously diminished and its degraded condition will have harmful effects throughout the landscape. It is this way with our symbolic environment. We have reached, I believe, a critical mass in that electronic media have decisively and irreversibly changed the character of our symbolic environment. We are now a culture whose information, ideas and epistemology are given form by television, not by the printed word. To be sure, there are still readers and there are many books published, but the uses of print and reading are not the same as they once were; not even in schools, the last institutions where print was thought to be invincible. They delude themselves who believe that television and print coexist, for coexistence implies parity. There is no parity here. Print is now merely a residual epistemology, and it will remain so, aided to some extent by the computer, and newspapers and magazines that are made to look like television screens. Like the fish who survive a toxic river and the boatmen who sail on it, there still dwell among us those whose sense of things is largely influenced by older and clearer waters.

The third point is that in the analogy I have drawn above, the river refers largely to what we call public discourse—our political, religious, informational and commercial forms of conversation. I am arguing that a television-based epistemology pollutes public communication and its surrounding landscape, not that it pollutes everything. In the first place, I am constantly reminded of television's value as a source of comfort and pleasure to the elderly, the infirm and, indeed, all people who find themselves alone in motel rooms. I am also aware of television's potential for creating a theater for the masses (a subject which in my opinion has not been taken seriously enough). There are also claims that whatever power television might have to undermine rational discourse, its emotional power is so great that it could arouse sentiment against the Vietnam War or against more virulent forms of racism. These and other beneficial possibilities are not to be taken lightly.

But there is still another reason why I should not like to be understood as making a total assault on television. Anyone who is even slightly familiar with the history of communications knows that every new technology for thinking involves a trade-off. It giveth and taketh away, although not quite in equal measure. Media change does not necessarily result in equilibrium. It sometimes creates more than it destroys. Sometimes, it is the other way around. We must be careful in praising or condemning because the future may hold surprises for us. The invention of the printing press itself is a paradigmatic example. Typography fostered the modern idea of individuality, but it destroyed the medieval sense of community and integration. Typography created prose but made poetry into an exotic and elitist form of expression. Typography made modern science possible but transformed religious sensibility into mere superstition. Typography assisted in the growth of the nation-state but thereby made patriotism into a sordid if not lethal emotion.

Obviously, my point of view is that the four-hundred-year imperial dominance of typography was of far greater benefit than deficit. Most of our modern ideas about the uses of the intellect were formed by the printed word, as were our ideas about education, knowledge, truth and information. I will try to demonstrate that as typography moves to the periphery of our culture and television takes its place at the center, the seriousness, clarity and, above all, value of public discourse dangerously declines. On what benefits may come from other directions, one must keep an open mind.

3.

Typographic America

In the *Autobiography of Benjamin Franklin*, there appears a remarkable quotation attributed to Michael Welfare, one of the founders of a religious sect known as the Dunkers and a longtime acquaintance of Franklin. The statement had its origins in Welfare's complaint to Franklin that zealots of other religious persuasions were spreading lies about the Dunkers, accusing them of abominable principles to which, in fact, they were utter strangers. Franklin suggested that such abuse might be diminished if the Dunkers published the articles of their belief and the rules of their discipline. Welfare replied that this course of action had been discussed among his co-religionists but had been rejected. He then explained their reasoning in the following words:

> When we were first drawn together as a society, it had pleased God to enlighten our minds so far as to see that some doctrines, which we once esteemed truths, were errors, and that others, which we had esteemed errors, were real truths. From time to time He has been pleased to afford us farther light, and our principles have been improving, and our errors diminishing. Now we are not sure that we are arrived at the end of this progression, and at the perfection of spiritual or theological knowledge; and we fear that, if we should feel ourselves as if bound and confined by it, and perhaps be unwilling to receive further improvement, and our successors still more so, as conceiving what we their elders and founders had done, to be something sacred, never to be departed from.[1]

30

Franklin describes this sentiment as a singular instance in the history of mankind of modesty in a sect. Modesty is certainly the word for it, but the statement is extraordinary for other reasons, too. We have here a criticism of the epistemology of the written word worthy of Plato. Moses himself might be interested although he could hardly approve. The Dunkers came close here to formulating a commandment about religious discourse: Thou shalt not write down thy principles, still less print them, lest thou shall be entrapped by them for all time.

We may, in any case, consider it a significant loss that we have no record of the deliberations of the Dunkers. It would certainly shed light on the premise of this book, i.e., that the form in which ideas are expressed affects what those ideas will be. But more important, their deliberations were in all likelihood a singular instance in Colonial America of a distrust of the printed word. For the Americans among whom Franklin lived were as committed to the printed word as any group of people who have ever lived. Whatever else may be said of those immigrants who came to settle in New England, it is a paramount fact that they and their heirs were dedicated and skillful readers whose religious sensibilities, political ideas and social life were embedded in the medium of typography.

We know that on the *Mayflower* itself several books were included as cargo, most importantly, the Bible and Captain John Smith's *Description of New England*. (For immigrants headed toward a largely uncharted land, we may suppose that the latter book was as carefully read as the former.) We know, too, that in the very first days of colonization each minister was given ten pounds with which to start a religious library. And although literacy rates are notoriously difficult to assess, there is sufficient evidence (mostly drawn from signatures) that between 1640 and 1700, the literacy rate for men in Massachusetts and Connecticut was somewhere between 89 percent and 95 percent, quite probably the highest concentration of literate males to be found anywhere in the world at that time.[2] (The literacy rate for women in those colonies is estimated to have run as high as 62 percent in the years 1681–1697.[3])

It is to be understood that the Bible was the central reading matter in all households, for these people were Protestants who shared Luther's belief that printing was "God's highest and extremest act of Grace, whereby the business of the Gospel is driven forward." Of course, the business of the Gospel may be driven forward in books other than the Bible, as for example in the famous *Bay Psalm Book*, printed in 1640 and generally regarded as America's first best seller. But it is not to be assumed that these people confined their reading to religious matters. Probate records indicate that 60 percent of the estates in Middlesex County between the years 1654 and 1699 contained books, all but 8 percent of them including more than the Bible.[4] In fact, between 1682 and 1685, Boston's leading bookseller imported 3,421 books from *one* English dealer, most of these nonreligious books. The meaning of this fact may be appreciated when one adds that these books were intended for consumption by approximately 75,000 people then living in the northern colonies.[5] The modern equivalent would be ten million books.

Aside from the fact that the religion of these Calvinist Puritans demanded that they be literate, three other factors account for the colonists' preoccupation with the printed word. Since the male literacy rate in seventeenth-century England did not exceed 40 percent, we may assume, first of all, that the migrants to New England came from more literate areas of England or from more literate segments of the population, or both.[6] In other words, they came here as readers and were certain to believe that reading was as important in the New World as it was in the Old. Second, from 1650 onward almost all New England towns passed laws requiring the maintenance of a "reading and writing" school, the large communities being required to maintain a grammar school, as well.[7] In all such laws, reference is made to Satan, whose evil designs, it was supposed, could be thwarted at every turn by education. But there were other reasons why education was required, as suggested by the following ditty, popular in the seventeenth century:

> *From public schools shall general*
> *knowledge flow,*
> *For 'tis the people's sacred*
> *right to know.*[8]

These people, in other words, had more than the subjection of Satan on their minds. Beginning in the sixteenth century, a great epistemological shift had taken place in which knowledge of every kind was transferred to, and made manifest through, the printed page. "More than any other device," Lewis Mumford wrote of this shift, "the printed book released people from the domination of the immediate and the local; . . . print made a greater impression than actual events. . . . To exist was to exist in print: the rest of the world tended gradually to become more shadowy. Learning became book-learning."[9] In light of this, we may assume that the schooling of the young was understood by the colonists not only as a moral duty but as an intellectual imperative. (The England from which they came was an island of schools. By 1660, for example, there were 444 schools in England, one school approximately every twelve miles.[10]) And it is clear that growth in literacy was closely connected to schooling. Where schooling was not required (as in Rhode Island) or weak school laws prevailed (as in New Hampshire), literacy rates increased more slowly than elsewhere.

Finally, these displaced Englishmen did not need to print their own books or even nurture their own writers. They imported, whole, a sophisticated literary tradition from their Motherland. In 1736, booksellers advertised the availability of the *Spectator*, the *Tatler*, and Steele's *Guardian*. In 1738, advertisements appeared for Locke's *Essay Concerning Human Understanding*, Pope's *Homer*, Swift's *A Tale of a Tub* and Dryden's

Fables.[11] Timothy Dwight, president of Yale University, described the American situation succinctly:

> Books of almost every kind, on almost every subject, are already written to our hands. Our situation in this respect is singular. As we speak the same language with the people of Great Britain, and have usually been at peace with that country; our commerce with it brings to us, regularly, not a small part of the books with which it is deluged. In every art, science, and path of literature, we obtain those, which to a great extent supply our wants.[12]

One significant implication of this situation is that no literary aristocracy emerged in Colonial America. Reading was not regarded as an elitist activity, and printed matter was spread evenly among all kinds of people. A thriving, classless reading culture developed because, as Daniel Boorstin writes, "It was diffuse. Its center was everywhere because it was nowhere. Every man was close to what [printed matter] talked about. Everyone could speak the same language. It was the product of a busy, mobile, public society."[13] By 1772, Jacob Duché could write: "The poorest labourer upon the shore of the Delaware thinks himself entitled to deliver his sentiment in matters of religion or politics with as much freedom as the gentleman or scholar. . . . Such is the prevailing taste for books of every kind, that almost every man is a reader."[14]

Where such a keen taste for books prevailed among the general population, we need not be surprised that Thomas Paine's *Common Sense,* published on January 10, 1776, sold more than 100,000 copies by March of the same year.[15] In 1985, a book would have to sell eight million copies (in two months) to match the proportion of the population Paine's book attracted. If we go beyond March, 1776, a more awesome set of figures is given by Howard Fast: "No one knows just how many copies were actually printed. The most conservative sources place the figure at something over 300,000 copies. Others place it just under half a million. Taking a figure of 400,000 in a population of 3,000,000, a book published today would have to sell 24,000,000 copies to do as well."[16] The only communication event that could produce such collective attention in today's America is the Superbowl.

It is worth pausing here for a moment to say something of Thomas Paine, for in an important way he is a measure of the high and wide level of literacy that existed in his time. In particular, I want to note that in spite of his lowly origins, no question has ever been raised, as it has with Shakespeare, about whether or not Paine was, in fact, the author of the works attributed to him. It is true that we know more of Paine's life than Shakespeare's (although not more of Paine's early periods), but it is also true that Paine had less formal schooling than Shakespeare, and came from the lowest laboring class before he arrived in America. In spite of these disadvantages, Paine wrote political philosophy and polemics the equal in lucidity and vitality (although not quantity) of Voltaire's, Rousseau's, and contemporary English philosophers', including Edmund Burke. Yet no one asked the question, How could an unschooled staymaker from England's impoverished class produce such stunning prose? From time to time Paine's lack of education was pointed out by his enemies (and he, himself, felt inferior because of this deficiency), but it was never doubted that such powers of written expression could originate from a common man.

It is also worth mentioning that the full title of Paine's most widely read book is *Common Sense, Written by an Englishman.* The tagline is important here because, as noted earlier, Americans did not write many books in the Colonial period, which Benjamin Franklin tried to explain by claiming that Americans were too busy doing other things. Perhaps so. But Americans were not too busy to make use of the printing press, even if not for books they themselves had written. The first printing press in America was established in 1638 as an adjunct of Harvard

University, which was two years old at the time.[17] Presses were established shortly thereafter in Boston and Philadelphia without resistance by the Crown, a curious fact since at this time presses were not permitted in Liverpool and Birmingham, among other English cities.[18] The earliest use of the press was for the printing of newsletters, mostly done on cheap paper. It may well be that the development of an American literature was retarded not by the industry of the people or the availability of English literature but by the scarcity of quality paper. As late as Revolutionary days, George Washington was forced to write to his generals on unsightly scraps of paper, and his dispatches were not enclosed in envelopes, paper being too scarce for such use.[19]

Yet by the late seventeenth century, there was a beginning to a native literature that turned out to have as much to do with the typographic bias of American culture as books. I refer, of course, to the newspaper, at which Americans first tried their hand on September 25, 1690, in Boston, when Benjamin Harris printed the first edition of a three-page paper he called *Publick Occurrences Both Foreign and Domestick.* Before he came to America, Harris had played a role in "exposing" a nonexistent conspiracy of Catholics to slaughter Protestants and burn London. His London newspaper, *Domestick Intelligence,* revealed the "Popish plot," with the result that Catholics were harshly persecuted.[20] Harris, no stranger to mendacity, indicated in his prospectus for *Publick Occurrences* that a newspaper was necessary to combat the spirit of lying which then prevailed in Boston and, I am told, still does. He concluded his prospectus with the following sentence: "It is suppos'd that none will dislike this Proposal but such as intend to be guilty of so villainous a crime." Harris was right about who would dislike his proposal. The second issue of *Publick Occurrences* never appeared. The Governor and Council suppressed it, complaining that Harris had printed "reflections of a very high nature,"[21] by which they meant that they had no intention of admitting any impediments to whatever villainy they wished to pursue. Thus, in the New World began the struggle for freedom of information which, in the Old, had begun a century before.

Harris' abortive effort inspired other attempts at newspaper publication: for example, the *Boston News-Letter*, published in 1704, generally regarded as the first continuously published American newspaper. This was followed by the *Boston Gazette* (in 1719) and the *New-England Courant* (in 1721), whose editor, James Franklin, was the older brother of Benjamin. By 1730, there were seven newspapers published regularly in four colonies, and by 1800 there were more than 180. In 1770, the *New York Gazette* congratulated itself and other papers by writing (in part):

> *'Tis truth (with deference to the college)*
> *Newspapers are the spring of Knowledge,*
> *The general source throughout the nation,*
> *Of every modern conversation.* [22]

At the end of the eighteenth century, the Reverend Samuel Miller boasted that the United States had more than two-thirds the number of newspapers available in England, and yet had only half the population of England. [23]

In 1786, Benjamin Franklin observed that Americans were so busy reading newspapers and pamphlets that they scarcely had time for books. (One book they apparently always had time for was Noah Webster's *American Spelling Book*, for it sold more than 24 million copies between 1783 and 1843.) [24] Franklin's reference to pamphlets ought not to go unnoticed. The proliferation of newspapers in all the Colonies was accompanied by the rapid diffusion of pamphlets and broadsides. Alexis de Tocqueville took note of this fact in his *Democracy in America,* published in 1835: "In America," he wrote, "parties do not write books to combat each other's opinions, but pamphlets, which are circulated for a day with incredible rapidity and then expire." [25] And he referred to both newspapers and pamphlets when he observed, "the invention of firearms equalized the vassal and the noble on the field of battle; the art of printing opened the same resources to the minds of all classes; the post brought knowledge alike to the door of the cottage and to the gate of the palace."[26]

At the time Tocqueville was making his observations of America, printing had already spread to all the regions of the country. The South had lagged behind the North not only in the formation of schools (almost all of which were private rather than public) but in its uses of the printing press. Virginia, for example, did not get its first regularly published newspaper, the *Virginia Gazette*, until 1736. But toward the end of the eighteenth century, the movement of ideas via the printed word was relatively rapid, and something approximating a national conversation emerged. For example, the *Federalist Papers*, an outpouring of eighty-five essays written by Alexander Hamilton, James Madison, and John Jay (all under the name of Publius) originally appeared in a New York newspaper during 1787 and 1788 but were read almost as widely in the South as the North.

As America moved into the nineteenth century, it did so as a fully print-based culture in all of its regions. Between 1825 and 1850, the number of subscription libraries trebled.[27] What were called "mechanics' and apprentices' libraries"—that is, libraries intended for the working class—also emerged as a force for literacy. In 1829, the New York Apprentices' Library housed ten thousand volumes, of which 1,600 apprentices drew books. By 1857, the same library served three-quarters of a million people.[28] Aided by Congress' lowering of the postal rates in 1851, the penny newspaper, the periodical, the Sunday school tract, and the cheaply bound book were abundantly available. Between 1836 and 1890, 107 million copies of the *McGuffey Reader* were distributed to the schools.[29] And although the reading of novels was not considered an altogether reputable use of time, Americans devoured them. Of Walter Scott's novels, published between 1814 and 1832, Samuel Goodrich wrote: "The appearance of a new novel from his pen caused a greater sensation in the United States than did some of the battles of Napoleon. . . . Everybody read these works; everybody—the refined and the simple."[30] Publishers were so anxious to make prospective best sellers available, they would sometimes dispatch messengers to incoming packet boats and "within a single day set up, printed and bound in paper covers the most recent novel of Bulwer or Dickens."[31] There being no international copyright laws, "pirated" editions abounded, with no complaint from the public, or much from authors, who were lionized. When Charles Dickens visited America in 1842, his reception equaled the adulation we offer today to television stars, quarterbacks, and Michael Jackson. "I can give you no conception of my welcome," Dickens wrote to a friend. "There never was a King or Emperor upon earth so cheered and followed by the crowds, and entertained at splendid balls and dinners and waited upon by public bodies of all kinds. . . . If I go out in a carriage, the crowd surrounds it and escorts me home; if I go to the theater, the whole house . . . rises as one man and the timbers ring again."[32] A native daughter, Harriet Beecher Stowe, was not offered the same kind of adoring attention—and, of course, in the South, had her carriage been surrounded, it would not have been for the purpose of escorting her home— but her *Uncle Tom's Cabin* sold 305,000 copies in its first year, the equivalent of four million in today's America.

Alexis de Tocqueville was not the only foreign visitor to be impressed by the Americans' immersion in printed matter. During the nineteenth century, scores of Englishmen came to America to see for themselves what had become of the Colonies. All were impressed with the high level of literacy and in particular its extension to all classes.[33]

In addition, they were astounded by the near universality of lecture halls in which stylized oral performance provided a continuous reinforcement of the print tradition. Many of these lecture halls originated as a result of the Lyceum Movement, a form of adult education. Usually associated with the efforts of Josiah Holbrook, a New England farmer, the Lyceum Movement had as its purpose the diffusion of knowledge, the promotion of common schools, the creation of libraries and, especially, the establishment of lecture halls. By 1835, there were more than three thousand Lyceums in fifteen states.[34] Most of these were located east of the Alleghenies, but by 1840, they were to be found at the edges of the frontier, as far west as Iowa and Minnesota. Alfred Bunn, an Englishman on an extensive tour through America, reported in 1853 that "practically every village had its lecture hall."[35] He added: "It is a matter of wonderment . . . to witness the youthful workmen, the over-tired artisan, the worn-out factory girl . . . rushing . . . after the toil of the day is over, into the hot atmosphere of a crowded lecture room."[36] Bunn's countryman J. F. W. Johnston attended lectures at this time at the Smithsonian Institution and "found the lecture halls jammed with capacity audiences of 1200 and 1500 people."[37] Among the lecturers these audiences could hear were the leading intellectuals, writers and humorists (who were also writers) of their time, including Henry Ward Beecher, Horace Greeley, Louis Agassiz and Ralph Waldo Emerson (whose fee for a lecture was fifty dollars).[38] In his autobiography, Mark Twain devotes two chapters to his experiences as a lecturer on the Lyceum circuit. "I began as a lecturer in 1866 in California and Nevada," he wrote. "[I] lectured in New York once and in the Mississippi Valley a few times; in 1868 [I] made the whole Western circuit; and in the two or three following seasons added the Eastern circuit to my route."[39] Apparently, Emerson was underpaid since Twain remarks that some lecturers charged as much as $250 when they spoke in towns and $400 when they spoke in cities (which is almost as much, in today's terms, as the going price for a lecture by a retired television newscaster).

The point all this is leading to is that from its beginning until

well into the nineteenth century, America was as dominated by
the printed word and an oratory based on the printed word as
any society we know of. This situation was only in part a legacy
of the Protestant tradition. As Richard Hofstadter reminds us,
America was founded by intellectuals, a rare occurrence in the
history of modern nations. "The Founding Fathers," he writes,
"were sages, scientists, men of broad cultivation, many of them
apt in classical learning, who used their wide reading in history,
politics, and law to solve the exigent problems of their time."[40]
A society shaped by such men does not easily move in contrary
directions. We might even say that America was founded by
intellectuals, from which it has taken us two centuries and a
communications revolution to recover. Hofstadter has written
convincingly of our efforts to "recover," that is to say, of the
anti-intellectual strain in American public life, but he concedes
that his focus distorts the general picture. It is akin to writing a
history of American business by concentrating on the history of
bankruptcies.[41]

The influence of the printed word in every arena of public
discourse was insistent and powerful not merely because of the
quantity of printed matter but because of its *monopoly*. This
point cannot be stressed enough, especially for those who are
reluctant to acknowledge profound differences in the media en-
vironments of then and now. One sometimes hears it said, for
example, that there is more printed matter available today than
ever before, which is undoubtedly true. But from the seventeenth century to the late nineteenth century, printed matter
was virtually *all* that was available. There were no movies to
see, radio to hear, photographic displays to look at, records to
play. There was no television. Public business was channeled
into and expressed through print, which became the model, the
metaphor and the measure of all discourse. The resonances of
the lineal, analytical structure of print, and in particular, of expository prose, could be felt everywhere. For example, in how
people talked. Tocqueville remarks on this in *Democracy in*

America. "An American," he wrote, "cannot converse, but he can discuss, and his talk falls into a dissertation. He speaks to you as if he was addressing a meeting; and if he should chance to become warm in the discussion, he will say 'Gentlemen' to the person with whom he is conversing."[42] This odd practice is less a reflection of an American's obstinacy than of his modeling his conversational style on the structure of the printed word. Since the printed word is impersonal and is addressed to an invisible audience, what Tocqueville is describing here is a kind of printed orality, which was observable in diverse forms of oral discourse. On the pulpit, for example, sermons were usually written speeches delivered in a stately, impersonal tone consisting "largely of an impassioned, coldly analytical cataloguing of the attributes of the Deity as revealed to man through Nature and Nature's Laws."[43] And even when The Great Awakening came—a revivalist movement that challenged the analytical, dispassionate spirit of Deism—its highly emotional preachers used an oratory that could be transformed easily to the printed page. The most charismatic of these men was the Reverend George Whitefield, who beginning in 1739 preached all over America to large crowds. In Philadelphia, he addressed an audience of ten thousand people, whom he deeply stirred and alarmed by assuring them of eternal hellfire if they refused to accept Christ. Benjamin Franklin witnessed one of Whitefield's performances and responded by offering to become his publisher. In due time, Whitefield's journals and sermons were published by B. Franklin of Philadelphia.[44]

But obviously I do not mean to say that print merely influenced the form of public discourse. That does not say much unless one connects it to the more important idea that form will determine the nature of content. For those readers who may believe that this idea is too "McLuhanesque" for their taste, I offer Karl Marx from *The German Ideology*. "Is the *Iliad* possible," he asks rhetorically, "when the printing press and even printing machines exist? Is it not inevitable that with the emergence of the press, the singing and the telling and the muse cease; that is, the conditions necessary for epic poetry disappear?''[45] Marx understood well that the press was not merely a machine but a structure for discourse, which both rules out and insists upon certain kinds of content and, inevitably, a certain kind of audience. He did not, himself, fully explore the matter, and others have taken up the task. I too must try my hand at it—to explore how the press worked as a metaphor and an epistemology to create a serious and rational public conversation, from which we have now been so dramatically separated.

4.

The Typographic Mind

The first of the seven famous debates between Abraham Lincoln and Stephen A. Douglas took place on August 21, 1858, in Ottowa, Illinois. Their arrangement provided that Douglas would speak first, for one hour; Lincoln would take an hour and a half to reply; Douglas, a half hour to rebut Lincoln's reply. This debate was considerably shorter than those to which the two men were accustomed. In fact, they had tangled several times before, and all of their encounters had been much lengthier and more exhausting. For example, on October 16, 1854, in Peoria, Illinois, Douglas delivered a three-hour address to which Lincoln, by agreement, was to respond. When Lincoln's turn came, he reminded the audience that it was already 5 p.m., that he would probably require as much time as Douglas and that Douglas was still scheduled for a rebuttal. He proposed, therefore, that the audience go home, have dinner, and return refreshed for four more hours of talk. [1] The audience amiably agreed, and matters proceeded as Lincoln had outlined.

What kind of audience was this? Who were these people who could so cheerfully accommodate themselves to seven hours of oratory? It should be noted, by the way, that Lincoln and Douglas were not presidential candidates; at the time of their encounter in Peoria they were not even candidates for the United States Senate. But their audiences were not especially concerned with their official status. These were people who regarded such events as essential to their political education, who took them to be an integral part of their social lives, and who were quite accustomed to extended oratorical performances. Typically at county or state fairs, programs included many speakers, most of whom were allotted three hours for their arguments. And since it was preferred that speakers not go unanswered, their opponents were allotted an equal length of time. (One might add that the speakers were not always men. At one fair lasting several days in Springfield, "Each evening a woman [lectured] in the courtroom on 'Woman's Influence in the Great Progressive Movements of the Day.'"[2])

Moreover, these people did not rely on fairs or special events to get their fill of oratory. The tradition of the "stump" speaker was widely practiced, especially in the western states. By the stump of a felled tree or some equivalent open space, a speaker would gather an audience, and, as the saying had it, "take the stump" for two or three hours. Although audiences were mostly respectful and attentive, they were not quiet or unemotional. Throughout the Lincoln-Douglas debates, for example, people shouted encouragement to the speakers ("You tell 'em, Abe!") or voiced terse expressions of scorn ("Answer that one, if you can"). Applause was frequent, usually reserved for a humorous or elegant phrase or a cogent point. At the first debate in Ottowa, Douglas responded to lengthy applause with a remarkable and revealing statement. "My friends," he said, "silence will be more acceptable to me in the discussion of these questions than applause. I desire to address myself to your judgment, your understanding, and your consciences, and not to your passions or your enthusiasms."[3] As to the conscience of the audience, or even its judgment, it is difficult to say very much. But as to its understanding, a great deal can be assumed.

For one thing, its attention span would obviously have been extraordinary by current standards. Is there any audience of Americans today who could endure seven hours of talk? or five? or three? Especially without pictures of any kind? Second, these audiences must have had an equally extraordinary capacity to comprehend lengthy and complex sentences aurally. In

Douglas' Ottowa speech he included in his one-hour address three long, legally phrased resolutions of the Abolition platform. Lincoln, in his reply, read even longer passages from a published speech he had delivered on a previous occasion. For all of Lincoln's celebrated economy of style, his sentence structure in the debates was intricate and subtle, as was Douglas'. In the second debate, at Freeport, Illinois, Lincoln rose to answer Douglas in the following words:

> It will readily occur to you that I cannot, in half an hour, notice all the things that so able a man as Judge Douglas can say in an hour and a half; and I hope, therefore, if there be anything that he has said upon which you would like to hear something from me, but which I omit to comment upon, you will bear in mind that it would be expecting an impossibility for me to cover his whole ground.[4]

It is hard to imagine the present occupant of the White House being capable of constructing such clauses in similar circumstances. And if he were, he would surely do so at the risk of burdening the comprehension or concentration of his audience. People of a television culture need "plain language" both aurally and visually, and will even go so far as to require it in some circumstances by law. The Gettysburg Address would probably have been largely incomprehensible to a 1985 audience.

The Lincoln-Douglas audience apparently had a considerable grasp of the issues being debated, including knowledge of historical events and complex political matters. At Ottowa, Douglas put seven interrogatives to Lincoln, all of which would have been rhetorically pointless unless the audience was familiar with the Dred Scott decision, the quarrel between Douglas and President Buchanan, the disaffection of some Democrats, the Abolition platform, and Lincoln's famous "House divided" speech at Cooper Union. Further, in answering Douglas' questions in a later debate, Lincoln made a subtle distinction between what he was, or was not, "pledged" to uphold and what he actually believed, which he surely would not have attempted unless he assumed the audience could grasp his point. Finally, while both speakers employed some of the more simpleminded weapons of argumentative language (e.g., name-calling and bombastic generalities), they consistently drew upon more complex rhetorical resources—sarcasm, irony, paradox, elaborated metaphors, fine distinctions and the exposure of contradiction, none of which would have advanced their respective causes unless the audience was fully aware of the means being employed.

It would be false, however, to give the impression that these 1858 audiences were models of intellectual propriety. All of the Lincoln-Douglas debates were conducted amid a carnival-like atmosphere. Bands played (although not during the debates), hawkers sold their wares, children romped, liquor was available. These were important social events as well as rhetorical performances, but this did not trivialize them. As I have indicated, these audiences were made up of people whose intellectual lives and public business were fully integrated into their social world. As Winthrop Hudson has pointed out, even Methodist camp meetings combined picnics with opportunities to listen to oratory.[5] Indeed, most of the camp grounds originally established for religious inspiration—Chautauqua, New York; Ocean Grove, New Jersey; Bayview, Michigan; Junaluska, North Carolina—were eventually transformed into conference centers, serving educational and intellectual functions. In other words, the use of language as a means of complex argument was an important, pleasurable and common form of discourse in almost every public arena.

To understand the audience to whom Lincoln and Douglas directed their memorable language, we must remember that these people were the grandsons and granddaughters of the Enlightenment (American version). They were the progeny of Franklin, Jefferson, Madison and Tom Paine, the inheritors of the Empire of Reason, as Henry Steele Commager has called eighteenth-century America. It is true that among their number were frontiersmen, some of whom were barely literate, and immigrants to whom English was still strange. It is also true that by 1858, the photograph and telegraph had been invented, the advance guard of a new epistemology that would put an end to the Empire of Reason. But this would not become evident until the twentieth century. At the time of the Lincoln-Douglas debates, America was in the middle years of its most glorious literary outpouring. In 1858, Edwin Markham was six years old; Mark Twain was twenty-three; Emily Dickinson, twenty-eight; Whitman and James Russell Lowell, thirty-nine; Thoreau, forty-one; Melville, forty-five; Whittier and Longfellow, fifty-one; Hawthorne and Emerson, fifty-four and fifty-five; Poe had died nine years before.

I choose the Lincoln-Douglas debates as a starting point for this chapter not only because they were the preeminent example of political discourse in the mid-nineteenth century but also because they illustrate the power of typography to control the character of that discourse. Both the speakers and their audience were habituated to a kind of oratory that may be described as literary. For all of the hoopla and socializing surrounding the event, the speakers had little to offer, and audiences little to expect, but language. And the language that was offered was clearly modeled on the style of the written word. To anyone who has read what Lincoln and Douglas said, this is obvious from beginning to end. The debates opened, in fact, with Douglas making the following introduction, highly characteristic of everything that was said afterward:

> Ladies and Gentlemen: I appear before you today for the purpose of discussing the leading political topics which now agitate the public mind. By an arrangement between Mr. Lincoln and myself, we are present here today for the purpose of having a joint discussion, as the representatives of the two great political parties of the

State and Union, upon the principles in issue between those parties, and this vast concourse of people shows the deep feeling
which pervades the public mind in regard to the questions divid-
ing us.[6]

This language is pure print. That the occasion required it to be
spoken aloud cannot obscure that fact. And that the audience
was able to process it through the ear is remarkable only to
people whose culture no longer resonates powerfully with the
printed word. Not only did Lincoln and Douglas write all their
speeches in advance, but they also planned their rebuttals in
writing. Even the spontaneous interactions between the speakers were expressed in a sentence structure, sentence length and
rhetorical organization which took their form from writing. To
be sure, there were elements of pure orality in their presenta-
tions. After all, neither speaker was indifferent to the moods of
the audiences. Nonetheless, the resonance of typography was
ever-present. Here was argument and counterargument, claim
and counterclaim, criticism of relevant texts, the most careful
scrutiny of the previously uttered sentences of one's opponent.
In short, the Lincoln-Douglas debates may be described as expository prose lifted whole from the printed page. That is the
meaning of Douglas' reproach to the audience. He claimed that
his appeal was to understanding and not to passion, as if the
audience were to be silent, reflective readers, and his language
the text which they must ponder. Which brings us, of course, to
the questions, What are the implications for public discourse of
a written, or typographic, metaphor? What is the character of
its content? What does it demand of the public? What uses
of the mind does it favor?

One must begin, I think, by pointing to the obvious fact that
the written word, and an oratory based upon it, *has a content:* a
semantic, paraphrasable, propositional content. This may
sound odd, but since I shall be arguing soon enough that much
of our discourse today has only a marginal propositional con-

tent, I must stress the point here. Whenever language is the principal medium of communication—especially language controlled by the rigors of print—an idea, a fact, a claim is the inevitable result. The idea may be banal, the fact irrelevant, the claim false, but there is no escape from meaning when language is the instrument guiding one's thought. Though one may accomplish it from time to time, it is very hard to say nothing when employing a written English sentence. What else is exposition good for? Words have very little to recommend them except as carriers of meaning. The shapes of written words are not especially interesting to look at. Even the sounds of sentences of spoken words are rarely engaging except when composed by those with extraordinary poetic gifts. If a sentence refuses to issue forth a fact, a request, a question, an assertion, an explanation, it is nonsense, a mere grammatical shell. As a consequence a language-centered discourse such as was characteristic of eighteenth- and nineteenth-century America tends to be both content-laden and serious, all the more so when it takes its form from print.

It is serious because meaning demands to be understood. A written sentence calls upon its author to say something, upon its reader to know the import of what is said. And when an author and reader are struggling with semantic meaning, they are engaged in the most serious challenge to the intellect. This is especially the case with the act of reading, for authors are not always trustworthy. They lie, they become confused, they overgeneralize, they abuse logic and, sometimes, common sense. The reader must come armed, in a serious state of intellectual readiness. This is not easy because he comes to the text alone. In reading, one's responses are isolated, one's intellect thrown back on its own resources. To be confronted by the cold abstractions of printed sentences is to look upon language bare, without the assistance of either beauty or community. Thus, reading is by its nature a serious business. It is also, of course, an essentially rational activity.

From Erasmus in the sixteenth century to Elizabeth Eisenstein in the twentieth, almost every scholar who has grappled with the question of what reading does to one's habits of mind has concluded that the process encourages rationality; that the sequential, propositional character of the written word fosters what Walter Ong calls the "analytic management of knowledge." To engage the written word means to follow a line of thought, which requires considerable powers of classifying, inference-making and reasoning. It means to uncover lies, confusions, and overgeneralizations, to detect abuses of logic and common sense. It also means to weigh ideas, to compare and contrast assertions, to connect one generalization to another. To accomplish this, one must achieve a certain distance from the words themselves, which is, in fact, encouraged by the isolated and impersonal text. That is why a good reader does not cheer an apt sentence or pause to applaud even an inspired paragraph. Analytic thought is too busy for that, and too detached.

I do not mean to imply that prior to the written word analytic thought was not possible. I am referring here not to the potentialities of the individual mind but to the predispositions of a cultural mind-set. In a culture dominated by print, public discourse tends to be characterized by a coherent, orderly arrangement of facts and ideas. The public for whom it is intended is generally competent to manage such discourse. In a print culture, writers make mistakes when they lie, contradict themselves, fail to support their generalizations, try to enforce illogical connections. In a print culture, readers make mistakes when they don't notice, or even worse, don't care.

In the eighteenth and nineteenth centuries, print put forward a definition of intelligence that gave priority to the objective, rational use of the mind and at the same time encouraged forms of public discourse with serious, logically ordered content. It is no accident that the Age of Reason was coexistent with the growth of a print culture, first in Europe and then in America. The spread of typography kindled the hope that the world and its manifold mysteries could at least be comprehended, predicted, controlled. It is in the eighteenth century that science—the preeminent example of the analytic management of knowledge—begins its refashioning of the world. It is in the eighteenth century that capitalism is demonstrated to be a rational and liberal system of economic life, that religious superstition comes under furious attack, that the divine right of kings is shown to be a mere prejudice, that the idea of continuous progress takes hold, and that the necessity of universal literacy through education becomes apparent.

Perhaps the most optimistic expression of everything that typography implied is contained in the following paragraph from John Stuart Mill's autobiography:

> So complete was my father's reliance on the influence of mankind, wherever [literacy] is allowed to reach them, that he felt as if all would be gained if the whole population were taught to read, if all sorts of opinions were allowed to be addressed to them by word and in writing, and if, by means of the suffrage, they could nominate a legislature to give effect to the opinion they adopted.[7]

This was, of course, a hope never quite realized. At no point in the history of England or America (or anyplace else) has the dominion of reason been so total as the elder Mill imagined typography would allow. Nonetheless, it is not difficult to demonstrate that in the eighteenth and nineteenth centuries, American public discourse, being rooted in the bias of the printed word, was serious, inclined toward rational argument and presentation, and, therefore, made up of meaningful content.

Let us take religious discourse as an illustration of this point. In the eighteenth century believers were as much influenced by the rationalist tradition as anyone else. The New World offered freedom of religion to all, which implied that no force other than reason itself could be employed to bring light to the unbeliever. "Here Deism will have its full chance," said Ezra Stiles in one of his famous sermons in 1783. "Nor need libertines [any] more to complain of being overcome by any weapons but the gentle, the powerful ones of argument and truth."[8]

Leaving aside the libertines, we know that the Deists were certainly given their full chance. It is quite probable, in fact, that the first four presidents of the United States were Deists. Jefferson, certainly, did not believe in the divinity of Jesus Christ and, while he was President, wrote a version of the Four Gospels from which he removed all references to "fantastic" events, retaining only the ethical content of Jesus' teaching. Legend has it that when Jefferson was elected President, old women hid their Bibles and shed tears. What they might have done had Tom Paine become President or been offered some high post in the government is hard to imagine. In *The Age of Reason*, Paine attacked the Bible and all subsequent Christian theology. Of Jesus Christ, Paine allowed that he was a virtuous and amiable man but charged that the stories of his divinity were absurd and profane, which, in the way of the rationalist, he tried to prove by a close textual analysis of the Bible. "All national institutions of churches," he wrote, "whether Jewish, Christian or Turkish, appear to me no other than human inventions, set up to terrify and enslave mankind, and monopolize power and profit."[9] Because of *The Age of Reason*, Paine lost his standing among the pantheon of Founding Fathers (and to this day is treated ambiguously in American history textbooks). But Ezra Stiles did not say that libertines and Deists would be *loved:* only that with reason as their jury, they would have their say in an open court. As indeed they did. Assisted by the initial enthusiasms evoked by the French Revolution, the Deist attack on churches as enemies of progress and on religious superstition as enemy of rationality became a popular movement.[10] The churches fought back, of course, and when Deism ceased to attract interest, they fought among themselves. Toward the mid-eighteenth century, Theodore Frelinghuysen and William Tennent led a revivalist movement among Presbyterians. They were followed by the three great figures associated with religious "awakenings" in America—Jonathan Edwards, George Whitefield, and, later in the nineteenth century, Charles Finney.

These men were spectacularly successful preachers, whose appeal reached regions of consciousness far beyond where reason rules. Of Whitefield, it was said that by merely pronouncing the word "Mesopotamia," he evoked tears in his audience. Perhaps that is why Henry Coswell remarked in 1839 that "religious mania is said to be the prevailing form of insanity in the United States."[11] Yet it is essential to bear in mind that quarrels over doctrine between the revivalist movements of the eighteenth and nineteenth centuries and the established churches fiercely opposed to them were argued in pamphlets and books in largely rational, logically ordered language. It would be a serious mistake to think of Billy Graham or any other television revivalist as a latter-day Jonathan Edwards or Charles Finney. Edwards was one of the most brilliant and creative minds ever produced by America. His contribution to aesthetic theory was almost as important as his contribution to theology. His interests were mostly academic; he spent long hours each day in his study. He did not speak to his audiences extemporaneously. He *read* his sermons, which were tightly knit and closely reasoned expositions of theological doctrine.[12] Audiences may have been moved emotionally by Edwards' language, but they were, first and foremost, required to understand it. Indeed Edwards' fame was largely a result of a book, *Faithful Narrative of the Surprising Work of God in the Conversion of Many Hundred Souls in Northampton*, published in 1737. A later book, *A Treatise Concerning Religious Affections*, published in 1746, is considered to be among the most remarkable psychological studies ever produced in America.

Unlike the principal figures in today's "great awakening"— Oral Roberts, Jerry Falwell, Jimmy Swaggart, et al.—yesterday's leaders of revivalist movements in America were men of learning, faith in reason, and generous expository gifts. Their disputes with the religious establishments were as much about theology and the nature of consciousness as they were about religious inspiration. Finney, for example, was no "backcountry rustic," as he was sometimes characterized by his doctrinal opponents.[13] He had been trained as a lawyer, wrote an important book on systematic theology, and ended his career as a professor at and then president of Oberlin College.

The doctrinal disputes among religionists not only were argued in carefully drawn exposition in the eighteenth century, but in the nineteenth century were settled by the extraordinary expedient of founding colleges. It is sometimes forgotten that the churches in America laid the foundation of our system of higher education. Harvard, of course, was established early—in 1636—for the purpose of providing learned ministers to the Congregational Church. And, sixty-five years later, when Congregationalists quarreled among themselves over doctrine, Yale College was founded to correct the lax influences of Harvard (and, to this day, claims it has the same burden). The strong intellectual strain of the Congregationalists was matched by other denominations, certainly in their passion for starting colleges. The Presbyterians founded, among other schools, the University of Tennessee in 1784, Washington and Jefferson in 1802 and Lafayette in 1826. The Baptists founded, among others, Colgate (1817), George Washington (1821), Furman (1826), Denison (1832) and Wake Forest (1834). The Episcopalians founded Hobart (1822), Trinity (1823) and Kenyon (1824). The Methodists founded eight colleges between 1830 and 1851, including Wesleyan, Emory, and Depauw. In addition to Harvard and Yale, the Congregationalists founded Williams (1793), Middlebury (1800), Amherst (1821) and Oberlin (1833).

If this preoccupation with literacy and learning be a "form of insanity," as Coswell said of religious life in America, then let there be more of it. In the eighteenth and nineteenth centuries, religious thought and institutions in America were dominated by an austere, learned, and intellectual form of discourse that is largely absent from religious life today. No clearer example of the difference between earlier and modern forms of public discourse can be found than in the contrast between the theological arguments of Jonathan Edwards and those of, say, Jerry Falwell, or Billy Graham, or Oral Roberts. The formidable content to Edwards' theology must inevitably engage the intellect; if there is such a content to the theology of the television evangelicals, they have not yet made it known.

The differences between the character of discourse in a print-based culture and the character of discourse in a television-based culture are also evident if one looks at the legal system.

In a print-based culture, lawyers tended to be well educated, devoted to reason, and capable of impressive expositional argument. It is a matter frequently overlooked in histories of America that in the eighteenth and nineteenth centuries, the legal profession represented "a sort of privileged body in the scale of intellect," as Tocqueville remarked. Folk heroes were made of some of those lawyers, like Sergeant Prentiss of Alabama, or "Honest" Abe Lincoln of Illinois, whose craftiness in manipulating juries was highly theatrical, not unlike television's version of a trial lawyer. But the great figures of American jurisprudence—John Marshall, Joseph Story, James Kent, David Hoffman, William Wirt and Daniel Webster—were models of intellectual elegance and devotion to rationality and scholarship. They believed that democracy, for all of its obvious virtues, posed the danger of releasing an undisciplined individualism. Their aspiration was to save civilization in America by "creating a rationality for the law." [14] As a consequence of this exalted view, they believed that law must not be merely a learned profession but a liberal one. The famous law professor Job Tyson argued that a lawyer must be familiar with the works of Seneca, Cicero, and Plato. [15] George Sharswood, perhaps envisioning the degraded state of legal education in the twentieth century, remarked in 1854 that to read law exclusively will damage the mind, "shackle it to the technicalities with which it has become so familiar, and disable it from taking enlarged and comprehensive views even of topics falling within its compass."[16]

The insistence on a liberal, rational and articulate legal mind was reinforced by the fact that America had a written constitution, as did all of its component states, and that law did not grow by chance but was explicitly formulated. A lawyer needed to be a writing and reading man par excellence, for reason was the principal authority upon which legal questions were to be decided. John Marshall was, of course, the great "paragon of reason, as vivid a symbol to the American imagination as Natty Bumppo."[17] He was the preeminent example of Typographic Man—detached, analytical, devoted to logic, abhorring contradiction. It was said of him that he never used analogy as a principal support of his arguments. Rather, he introduced most of his decisions with the phrase "It is admitted. . . ." Once one admitted his premises, one was usually forced to accept his conclusion.

To an extent difficult to imagine today, earlier Americans were familiar not only with the great legal issues of their time but even with the language famous lawyers had used to argue their cases. This was especially true of Daniel Webster, and it was only natural that Stephen Vincent Benét in his famous short story would have chosen Daniel Webster to contend with the Devil. How could the Devil triumph over a man whose language, described by Supreme Court Justice Joseph Story, had the following characteristics?

> . . . his clearness and downright simplicity of statement, his vast comprehensiveness of topics, his fertility in illustrations drawn from practical sources; his keen analysis, and suggestion of difficulties; his power of disentangling a complicated proposition, and resolving it in elements so plain as to reach the most common minds; his vigor in generalizations, planting his own arguments behind the whole battery of his opponents; his wariness and cau-

tion not to betray himself by heat into untenable positions, or to spread his forces over useless ground.[18]

I quote this in full because it is the best nineteenth-century description I know of the character of discourse expected of one whose mind is formed by the printed word. It is exactly the ideal and model James Mill had in mind in prophesying about the wonders of typography. And if the model was somewhat unreachable, it stood nonetheless as an ideal to which every lawyer aspired.

Such an ideal went far beyond the legal profession or the ministry in its influence. Even in the everyday world of commerce, the resonances of rational, typographic discourse were to be found. If we may take advertising to be the voice of commerce, then its history tells very clearly that in the eighteenth and nineteenth centuries those with products to sell took their customers to be not unlike Daniel Webster: they assumed that potential buyers were literate, rational, analytical. Indeed, the history of newspaper advertising in America may be considered, all by itself, as a metaphor of the descent of the typographic mind, beginning, as it does, with reason, and ending, as it does, with entertainment. In Frank Presbrey's classic study *The History and Development of Advertising,* he discusses the decline of typography, dating its demise in the late 1860's and early 1870's. He refers to the period before then as the "dark ages" of typographical display.[19] The dark ages to which he refers began in 1704 when the first paid advertisements appeared in an American newspaper, *The Boston News-Letter.* These were three in number, occupying altogether four inches of single-column space. One of them offered a reward for the capture of a thief; another offered a reward for the return of an anvil that was "taken up" by some unknown party. The third actually offered something for sale, and, in fact, is not unlike real estate advertisements one might see in today's *New York Times:*

At Oysterbay, on *Long Island* in the Province of N. York. There is a very good Fulling-Mill, to be Let or Sold, as also a Plantation, having on it a large new Brick house, and another good house by it for a Kitchen & workhouse, with a Barn, Stable &c. a young Orchard and 20 acres clear land. The Mill is to be Let with or without the Plantation; Enquire of Mr. William *Bradford* Printer in N. York, and know further.[20]

For more than a century and a half afterward, advertisements took this form with minor alterations. For example, sixty-four years after Mr. Bradford advertised an estate in Oyster Bay, the legendary Paul Revere placed the following advertisement in the *Boston Gazette:*

Whereas many persons are so unfortunate as to lose their Fore-Teeth by Accident, and otherways, to their great Detriment, not only in Looks, but Speaking both in Public and Private:—This is to inform all such, that they may have them re-placed with false Ones, that look as well as the Natural, and Answers the End of Speaking to all Intents, by PAUL REVERE, Goldsmith, near the Head of Dr. Clarke's Wharf, Boston.[21]

Revere went on to explain in another paragraph that those whose false teeth had been fitted by John Baker, and who had suffered the indignity of having them loosen, might come to Revere to have them tightened. He indicated that he had learned how to do this from John Baker himself.

Not until almost a hundred years after Revere's announcement were there any serious attempts by advertisers to overcome the lineal, typographic form demanded by publishers.[22] And not until the end of the nineteenth century did advertising move fully into its modern mode of discourse. As late as 1890, advertising, still understood to consist of words, was regarded as an essentially serious and rational enterprise whose purpose was to convey information and make claims in propositional form. Advertising was, as Stephen Douglas said in another context, intended to appeal to understanding, not to passions. This is not to say that during the period of typographic display, the claims that were put forward were true. Words cannot guarantee their truth content. Rather, they assemble a context in which the question, Is this true or false? is relevant. In the 1890's that context was shattered, first by the massive intrusion of illustrations and photographs, then by the nonpropositional use of language. For example, in the 1890's advertisers adopted the technique of using slogans. Presbrey contends that modern advertising can be said to begin with the use of two such slogans: "You press the button; we do the rest" and "See that hump?" At about the same time, jingles started to be used, and in 1892, Procter and Gamble invited the public to submit rhymes to advertise Ivory Soap. In 1896, H-O employed, for the first time, a picture of a baby in a high chair, the bowl of cereal before him, his spoon in hand, his face ecstatic. By the turn of the century, advertisers no longer assumed rationality on the part of their potential customers. Advertising became one part depth psychology, one part aesthetic theory. Reason had to move itself to other arenas.

To understand the role that the printed word played in providing an earlier America with its assumptions about intelligence, truth and the nature of discourse, one must keep in view that the act of reading in the eighteenth and nineteenth centuries had an entirely different quality to it than the act of reading does today. For one thing, as I have said, the printed word had a monopoly on both attention and intellect, there being no other means, besides the oral tradition, to have access to public knowledge. Public figures were known largely by their written words, for example, not by their looks or even their oratory. It is quite likely that most of the first fifteen presidents of the United States would not have been recognized had they passed the average citizen in the street. This would have been the case as well of the great lawyers, ministers and scientists of that era. To

think about those men was to think about what they had written, to judge them by their public positions, their arguments,
their knowledge as codified in the printed word. You may get
some sense of how we are separated from this kind of consciousness by thinking about any of our recent presidents; or
even preachers, lawyers and scientists who are or who have
recently been public figures. Think of Richard Nixon or Jimmy
Carter or Billy Graham, or even Albert Einstein, and what will
come to your mind is an image, a picture of a face, most likely a
face on a television screen (in Einstein's case, a photograph of a
face). Of words, almost nothing will come to mind. This is the
difference between thinking in a word-centered culture and
thinking in an image-centered culture.

It is also the difference between living in a culture that provides little opportunity for leisure, and one that provides much.
The farm boy following the plow with book in hand, the
mother reading aloud to her family on a Sunday afternoon, the
merchant reading announcements of the latest clipper arrivals
—these were different kinds of readers from those of today.
There would have been little casual reading, for there was not a
great deal of time for that. Reading would have had a sacred
element in it, or if not that, would have at least occurred as a
daily or weekly ritual invested with special meaning. For we
must also remember that this was a culture without electricity.
It would not have been easy to read by either candlelight or,
later, gaslight. Doubtless, much reading was done between
dawn and the start of the day's business. What reading would
have been done was done seriously, intensely, and with steadfast purpose. The modern idea of testing a reader's "comprehension," as distinct from something else a reader may be
doing, would have seemed an absurdity in 1790 or 1830 or
1860. What else was reading but comprehending? As far as we
know, there did not exist such a thing as a "reading problem,"
except, of course, for those who could not attend school. To
attend school meant to learn to read, for without that capacity,

one could not participate in the culture's conversations. But most people could read and did participate. To these people, reading was both their connection to and their model of the world. The printed page revealed the world, line by line, page by page, to be a serious, coherent place, capable of management by reason, and of improvement by logical and relevant criticism.

Almost anywhere one looks in the eighteenth and nineteenth centuries, then, one finds the resonances of the printed word and, in particular, its inextricable relationship to all forms of public expression. It may be true, as Charles Beard wrote, that the primary motivation of the writers of the United States Constitution was the protection of their economic interests. But it is also true that they assumed that participation in public life required the capacity to negotiate the printed word. To them, mature citizenship was not conceivable without sophisticated literacy, which is why the voting age in most states was set at twenty-one, and why Jefferson saw in universal education America's best hope. And that is also why, as Allan Nevins and Henry Steele Commager have pointed out, the voting restrictions against those who owned no property were frequently overlooked, but not one's inability to read.

It may be true, as Frederick Jackson Turner wrote, that the spirit that fired the American mind was the fact of an ever-expanding frontier. But it is also true, as Paul Anderson has written, that "it is no mere figure of speech to say that farm boys followed the plow with book in hand, be it Shakespeare, Emerson, or Thoreau."[23] For it was not only a frontier mentality that led Kansas to be the first state to permit women to vote in school elections, or Wyoming the first state to grant complete equality in the franchise. Women were probably more adept readers than men, and even in the frontier states the principal means of public discourse issued from the printed word. Those who could read had, inevitably, to become part of the conversation.

It may also be true, as Perry Miller has suggested, that the religious fervor of Americans provided much of their energy; or, as earlier historians told it, that America was created by an idea whose time had come. I quarrel with none of these explanations. I merely observe that the America they try to explain was dominated by a public discourse which took its form from the products of the printing press. For two centuries, America declared its intentions, expressed its ideology, designed its laws, sold its products, created its literature and addressed its deities with black squiggles on white paper. It did its talking in typography, and with that as the main feature of its symbolic environment rose to prominence in world civilization.

The name I give to that period of time during which the American mind submitted itself to the sovereignty of the printing press is the Age of Exposition. Exposition is a mode of thought, a method of learning, and a means of expression. Almost all of the characteristics we associate with mature discourse were amplified by typography, which has the strongest possible bias toward exposition: a sophisticated ability to think conceptually, deductively and sequentially; a high valuation of reason and order; an abhorrence of contradiction; a large capacity for detachment and objectivity; and a tolerance for delayed response. Toward the end of the nineteenth century, for reasons I am most anxious to explain, the Age of Exposition began to pass, and the early signs of its replacement could be discerned. Its replacement was to be the Age of Show Business.

5.

The Peek-a-Boo World

Toward the middle years of the nineteenth century, two ideas came together whose convergence provided twentieth-century America with a new metaphor of public discourse. Their partnership overwhelmed the Age of Exposition, and laid the foundation for the Age of Show Business. One of the ideas was quite new, the other as old as the cave paintings of Altamira. We shall come to the old idea presently. The new idea was that transportation and communication could be disengaged from each other, that space was not an inevitable constraint on the movement of information.

Americans of the 1800's were very much concerned with the problem of "conquering" space. By the mid-nineteenth century, the frontier extended to the Pacific Ocean, and a rudimentary railroad system, begun in the 1830's, had started to move people and merchandise across the continent. But until the 1840's, information could move only as fast as a human being could carry it; to be precise, only as fast as a train could travel, which, to be even more precise, meant about thirty-five miles per hour. In the face of such a limitation, the development of America as a national community was retarded. In the 1840's, America was still a composite of regions, each conversing in its own ways, addressing its own interests. A continentwide conversation was not yet possible.

The solution to these problems, as every school child used to know, was electricity. To no one's surprise, it was an American who found a practical way to put electricity in the service of communication and, in doing so, eliminated the problem of space once and for all. I refer, of course, to Samuel Finley Breese Morse, America's first true "spaceman." His telegraph erased state lines, collapsed regions, and, by wrapping the continent in an information grid, created the possibility of a unified American discourse.

But at a considerable cost. For telegraphy did something that Morse did not foresee when he prophesied that telegraphy would make "one neighborhood of the whole country." It destroyed the prevailing definition of information, and in doing so gave a new meaning to public discourse. Among the few who understood this consequence was Henry David Thoreau, who remarked in *Walden* that "We are in great haste to construct a magnetic telegraph from Maine to Texas; but Maine and Texas, it may be, have nothing important to communicate. . . . We are eager to tunnel under the Atlantic and bring the old world some weeks nearer to the new; but perchance the first news that will leak through into the broad flapping American ear will be that Princess Adelaide has the whooping cough." [1]

Thoreau, as it turned out, was precisely correct. He grasped that the telegraph would create its own definition of discourse; that it would not only permit but insist upon a conversation between Maine and Texas; and that it would require the content of that conversation to be different from what Typographic Man was accustomed to.

The telegraph made a three-pronged attack on typography's definition of discourse, introducing on a large scale irrelevance, impotence, and incoherence. These demons of discourse were aroused by the fact that telegraphy gave a form of legitimacy to the idea of context-free information; that is, to the idea that the value of information need not be tied to any function it might serve in social and political decision-making and action, but may attach merely to its novelty, interest, and curiosity. The telegraph made information into a commodity, a "thing" that could be bought and sold irrespective of its uses or meaning.

But it did not do so alone. The potential of the telegraph to transform information into a commodity might never have been realized, except for the partnership between the telegraph and the press. The penny newspaper, emerging slightly before telegraphy, in the 1830's, had already begun the process of elevating irrelevance to the status of news. Such papers as Benjamin Day's *New York Sun* and James Bennett's *New York Herald* turned away from the tradition of news as reasoned (if biased) political opinion and urgent commercial information and filled their pages with accounts of sensational events, mostly concerning crime and sex. While such "human interest news" played little role in shaping the decisions and actions of readers, it was at least local—about places and people within their experience—and it was not always tied to the moment. The human-interest stories of the penny newspapers had a timeless quality; their power to engage lay not so much in their currency as in their transcendence. Nor did all newspapers occupy themselves with such content. For the most part, the information they provided was not only local but largely functional—tied to the problems and decisions readers had to address in order to manage their personal and community affairs.

The telegraph changed all that, and with astonishing speed. Within months of Morse's first public demonstration, the local and the timeless had lost their central position in newspapers, eclipsed by the dazzle of distance and speed. In fact, the first known use of the telegraph by a newspaper occurred *one day* after Morse gave his historic demonstration of telegraphy's workability. Using the same Washington-to-Baltimore line Morse had constructed, the *Baltimore Patriot* gave its readers information about action taken by the House of Representatives on the Oregon issue. The paper concluded its report by noting: ". . . we are thus enabled to give our readers information from Washington up to two o'clock. This is indeed the annihilation of space." [2]

For a brief time, practical problems (mostly involving the

scarcity of telegraph lines) preserved something of the old definition of news as functional information. But the foresighted among the nation's publishers were quick to see where the future lay, and committed their full resources to the wiring of the continent. William Swain, the owner of the *Philadelphia Public Ledger*, not only invested heavily in the Magnetic Telegraph Company, the first commercial telegraph corporation, but became its president in 1850.

It was not long until the fortunes of newspapers came to depend not on the quality or utility of the news they provided, but on how much, from what distances, and at what speed. James Bennett of the *New York Herald* boasted that in the first week of 1848, his paper contained 79,000 words of telegraphic content [3]—of what relevance to his readers, he didn't say. Only four years after Morse opened the nation's first telegraph line on May 24, 1844, the Associated Press was founded, and news from nowhere, addressed to no one in particular, began to crisscross the nation. Wars, crimes, crashes, fires, floods—much of it the social and political equivalent of Adelaide's whooping cough—became the content of what people called "the news of the day."

As Thoreau implied, telegraphy made relevance irrelevant. The abundant flow of information had very little or nothing to do with those to whom it was addressed; that is, with any social or intellectual context in which their lives were embedded. Coleridge's famous line about water everywhere without a drop to drink may serve as a metaphor of a decontextualized information environment: In a sea of information, there was very little of it to use. A man in Maine and a man in Texas could converse, but not about anything either of them knew or cared very much about. The telegraph may have made the country into "one neighborhood," but it was a peculiar one, populated by strangers who knew nothing but the most superficial facts about each other.

Since we live today in just such a neighborhood (now sometimes called a "global village"), you may get a sense of what is meant by context-free information by asking yourself the following question: How often does it occur that information provided you on morning radio or television, or in the morning newspaper, causes you to alter your plans for the day, or to take some action you would not otherwise have taken, or provides insight into some problem you are required to solve? For most of us, news of the weather will sometimes have such consequences; for investors, news of the stock market; perhaps an occasional story about a crime will do it, if by chance the crime occurred near where you live or involved someone you know. But most of our daily news is inert, consisting of information that gives us something to talk about but cannot lead to any meaningful action. This fact is the principal legacy of the telegraph: By generating an abundance of irrelevant information, it dramatically altered what may be called the "information-action ratio."

In both oral and typographic cultures, information derives its importance from the possibilities of action. Of course, in any communication environment, input (what one is informed about) always exceeds output (the possibilities of action based on information). But the situation created by telegraphy, and then exacerbated by later technologies, made the relationship between information and action both abstract and remote. For the first time in human history, people were faced with the problem of information glut, which means that simultaneously they were faced with the problem of a diminished social and political potency.

You may get a sense of what this means by asking yourself another series of questions: What steps do you plan to take to reduce the conflict in the Middle East? Or the rates of inflation, crime and unemployment? What are your plans for preserving the environment or reducing the risk of nuclear war? What do you plan to do about NATO, OPEC, the CIA, affirmative action, and the monstrous treatment of the Baha'is in Iran? I shall take the liberty of answering for you: You plan to do nothing about them. You may, of course, cast a ballot for someone who claims to have some plans, as well as the power to act. But this you can do only once every two or four years by giving one hour of your time, hardly a satisfying means of expressing the broad range of opinions you hold. Voting, we might even say, is the next to last refuge of the politically impotent. The last refuge is, of course, giving your opinion to a pollster, who will get a version of it through a desiccated question, and then will submerge it in a Niagara of similar opinions, and convert them into—what else?—another piece of news. Thus, we have here a great loop of impotence: The news elicits from you a variety of opinions about which you can do nothing except to offer them as more news, about which you can do nothing.

Prior to the age of telegraphy, the information-action ratio was sufficiently close so that most people had a sense of being able to control some of the contingencies in their lives. What people knew about had action-value. In the information world created by telegraphy, this sense of potency was lost, precisely because the whole world became the context for news. Everything became everyone's business. For the first time, we were sent information which answered no question we had asked, and which, in any case, did not permit the right of reply.

We may say then that the contribution of the telegraph to public discourse was to dignify irrelevance and amplify impotence. But this was not all: Telegraphy also made public discourse essentially incoherent. It brought into being a world of broken time and broken attention, to use Lewis Mumford's phrase. The principal strength of the telegraph was its capacity to move information, not collect it, explain it or analyze it. In this respect, telegraphy was the exact opposite of typography. Books, for example, are an excellent container for the accumulation, quiet scrutiny and organized analysis of information and ideas. It takes time to write a book, and to read one; time to discuss its contents and to make judgments about their merit, including the form of their presentation. A book is an attempt to make thought permanent and to contribute to the great conversation conducted by authors of the past. Therefore, civilized people everywhere consider the burning of a book a vile form of anti-intellectualism. *But the telegraph demands that we burn its contents.* The value of telegraphy is undermined by applying the tests of permanence, continuity or coherence. The telegraph is suited only to the flashing of messages, each to be quickly replaced by a more up-to-date message. Facts push other facts into and then out of consciousness at speeds that neither permit nor require evaluation.

The telegraph introduced a kind of public conversation whose form had startling characteristics: Its language was the language of headlines—sensational, fragmented, impersonal. News took the form of slogans, to be noted with excitement, to be forgotten with dispatch. Its language was also entirely discontinuous. One message had no connection to that which preceded or followed it. Each "headline" stood alone as its own context. The receiver of the news had to provide a meaning if he could. The sender was under no obligation to do so. And because of all this, the world as depicted by the telegraph began to appear unmanageable, even undecipherable. The line-by-line, sequential, continuous form of the printed page slowly began to lose its resonance as a metaphor of how knowledge was to be acquired and how the world was to be understood. "Knowing" the facts took on a new meaning, for it did not imply that one understood implications, background, or connections. Telegraphic discourse permitted no time for historical perspectives and gave no priority to the qualitative. To the telegraph, intelligence meant knowing *of* lots of things, not knowing *about* them.

Thus, to the reverent question posed by Morse—What hath God wrought?—a disturbing answer came back: a neighborhood of strangers and pointless quantity; a world of fragments and discontinuities. God, of course, had nothing to do with it.

And yet, for all of the power of the telegraph, had it stood alone as a new metaphor for discourse, it is likely that print culture would have withstood its assault; would, at least, have held its ground. As it happened, at almost exactly the same time Morse was reconceiving the meaning of information, Louis Daguerre was reconceiving the meaning of nature; one might even say, of reality itself. As Daguerre remarked in 1838 in a notice designed to attract investors, "The daguerreotype is not merely an instrument which serves to draw nature . . . [it] gives her the power to reproduce herself."[4]

Of course both the need and the power to draw nature have always implied reproducing nature, refashioning it to make it comprehensible and manageable. The earliest cave paintings were quite possibly visual projections of a hunt that had not yet taken place, wish fulfillments of an anticipated subjection of nature. Reproducing nature, in other words, is a very old idea. But Daguerre did not have this meaning of "reproduce" in mind. He meant to announce that the photograph would invest everyone with the power to duplicate nature as often and wherever one liked. He meant to say he had invented the world's first "cloning" device, that the photograph was to visual experience what the printing press was to the written word.

In point of fact, the daguerreotype was not quite capable of achieving such an equation. It was not until William Henry Fox Talbot, an English mathematician and linguist, invented the process of preparing a negative from which any number of positives could be made that the mass printing and publication of photographs became possible.[5] The name "photography" was given to this process by the famous astronomer Sir John F. W. Herschel. It is an odd name since it literally means "writing with light." Perhaps Herschel meant the name to be taken ironically, since it must have been clear from the beginning that photography and writing (in fact, language in any form) do not inhabit the same universe of discourse.

Nonetheless, ever since the process was named it has been

the custom to speak of photography as a "language." The metaphor is risky because it tends to obscure the fundamental differences between the two modes of conversation. To begin with, photography is a language that speaks only in particularities. Its vocabulary of images is limited to concrete representation. Unlike words and sentences, the photograph does not present to us an idea or concept about the world, except as we use language itself to convert the image to idea. By itself, a photograph cannot deal with the unseen, the remote, the internal, the abstract. It does not speak of "man," only of *a* man; not of "tree," only of *a* tree. You cannot produce a photograph of "nature," any more than a photograph of "the sea." You can only photograph a particular fragment of the here-and-now—a cliff of a certain terrain, in a certain condition of light; a wave at a moment in time, from a particular point of view. And just as "nature" and "the sea" cannot be photographed, such larger abstractions as truth, honor, love, falsehood cannot be talked about in the lexicon of pictures. For "showing of" and "talking about" are two very different kinds of processes. "Pictures," Gavriel Salomon has written, "need to be recognized, words need to be understood."[6] By this he means that the photograph presents the world as object; language, the world as idea. For even the simplest act of naming a thing is an act of thinking—of comparing one thing with others, selecting certain features in common, ignoring what is different, and making an imaginary category. There is no such thing in nature as "man" or "tree." The universe offers no such categories or simplifications; only flux and infinite variety. The photograph documents and celebrates the particularities of this infinite variety. Language makes them comprehensible.

The photograph also lacks a syntax, which deprives it of a capacity to argue with the world. As an "objective" slice of space-time, the photograph testifies that someone was there or something happened. Its testimony is powerful but it offers no opinions—no "should-have-beens" or "might-have-beens."

Photography is preeminently a world of fact, not of dispute about facts or of conclusions to be drawn from them. But this is not to say photography lacks an epistemological bias. As Susan Sontag has observed, a photograph implies "that we know about the world if we accept it as the camera records it."[7] But, as she further observes, all understanding begins with our *not* accepting the world as it appears. Language, of course, is the medium we use to challenge, dispute, and cross-examine what comes into view, what is on the surface. The words "true" and "false" come from the universe of language, and no other. When applied to a photograph, the question, Is it true? means only, Is this a reproduction of a real slice of space-time? If the answer is "Yes," there are no grounds for argument, for it makes no sense to disagree with an unfaked photograph. The photograph itself makes no arguable propositions, makes no extended and unambiguous commentary. It offers no assertions to refute, so it is not refutable.

The way in which the photograph records experience is also different from the way of language. Language makes sense only when it is presented as a sequence of propositions. Meaning is distorted when a word or sentence is, as we say, taken out of context; when a reader or listener is deprived of what was said before, and after. But there is no such thing as a photograph taken out of context, for a photograph does not require one. In fact, the point of photography is to isolate images from context, so as to make them visible in a different way. In a world of photographic images, Ms. Sontag writes, "all borders . . . seem arbitrary. Anything can be separated, can be made discontinuous, from anything else: All that is necessary is to frame the subject differently."[8] She is remarking on the capacity of photographs to perform a peculiar kind of dismembering of reality, a wrenching of moments out of their contexts, and a juxtaposing of events and things that have no logical or historical connection with each other. Like telegraphy, photography recreates the world as a series of idiosyncratic events. There is no beginning, middle, or end in a world of photographs, as there is none implied by telegraphy. The world is atomized. There is only a present and it need not be part of any story that can be told.

That the image and the word have different functions, work at different levels of abstraction, and require different modes of response will not come as a new idea to anyone. Painting is at least three times as old as writing, and the place of imagery in the repertoire of communication instruments was quite well understood in the nineteenth century. What was new in the mid-nineteenth century was the sudden and massive intrusion of the photograph and other iconographs into the symbolic environment. This event is what Daniel Boorstin in his pioneering book *The Image* calls "the graphic revolution." By this phrase, Boorstin means to call attention to the fierce assault on language made by forms of mechanically reproduced imagery that spread unchecked throughout American culture—photographs, prints, posters, drawings, advertisements. I choose the word "assault" deliberately here, to amplify the point implied in Boorstin's "graphic *revolution.*" The new imagery, with photography at its forefront, did not merely function as a supplement to language, but bid to replace it as our dominant means for construing, understanding, and testing reality. What Boorstin implies about the graphic revolution, I wish to make explicit here: The new focus on the image undermined traditional definitions of information, of news, and, to a large extent, of reality itself. First in billboards, posters, and advertisements, and later in such "news" magazines and papers as *Life, Look,* the New York *Daily Mirror* and *Daily News,* the picture forced exposition into the background, and in some instances obliterated it altogether. By the end of the nineteenth century, advertisers and newspapermen had discovered that a picture was not only worth a thousand words, but, where sales were concerned, was better. For countless Americans, seeing, not reading, became the basis for believing.

In a peculiar way, the photograph was the perfect complement to the flood of telegraphic news-from-nowhere that threatened to submerge readers in a sea of facts from unknown places about strangers with unknown faces. For the photograph gave a concrete reality to the strange-sounding datelines, and attached faces to the unknown names. Thus it provided the illusion, at least, that "the news" had a connection to something within one's sensory experience. It created an apparent context for the "news of the day." And the "news of the day" created a context for the photograph.

But the sense of context created by the partnership of photograph and headline was, of course, entirely illusory. You may get a better sense of what I mean here if you imagine a stranger's informing you that the illyx is a subspecies of vermiform plant with articulated leaves that flowers biannually on the island of Aldononjes. And if you wonder aloud, "Yes, but what has that to do with anything?" imagine that your informant replies, "But here is a photograph I want you to see," and hands you a picture labeled *Illyx on Aldononjes*. "Ah, yes," you might murmur, "now I see." It is true enough that the photograph provides a context for the sentence you have been given, and that the sentence provides a context of sorts for the photograph, and you may even believe for a day or so that you have learned something. But if the event is entirely self-contained, devoid of any relationship to your past knowledge or future plans, if that is the beginning and end of your encounter with the stranger, then the appearance of context provided by the conjunction of sentence and image is illusory, and so is the impression of meaning attached to it. You will, in fact, have "learned" nothing (except perhaps to avoid strangers with photographs), and the illyx will fade from your mental landscape as though it had never been. At best you are left with an amusing bit of trivia, good for trading in cocktail party chatter or solving a crossword puzzle, but nothing more.

It may be of some interest to note, in this connection, that the crossword puzzle became a popular form of diversion in America at just that point when the telegraph and the photograph had achieved the transformation of news from functional information to decontextualized fact. This coincidence suggests that the new technologies had turned the age-old problem of information on its head: Where people once sought information to manage the real contexts of their lives, now they had to invent contexts in which otherwise useless information might be put to some apparent use. The crossword puzzle is one such pseudo-context; the cocktail party is another; the radio quiz shows of the 1930's and 1940's and the modern television game show are still others; and the ultimate, perhaps, is the wildly successful "Trivial Pursuit." In one form or another, each of these supplies an answer to the question, "What am I to do with all these disconnected facts?" And in one form or another, the answer is the same: Why not use them for diversion? for entertainment? to amuse yourself, in a game? In *The Image*, Boorstin calls the major creation of the graphic revolution the "pseudo-event," by which he means an event specifically staged to be reported—like the press conference, say. I mean to suggest here that a more significant legacy of the telegraph and the photograph may be the pseudo-*context*. A pseudo-context is a structure invented to give fragmented and irrelevant information a seeming use. But the use the pseudo-context provides is not action, or problem-solving, or change. It is the only use left for information with no genuine connection to our lives. And that, of course, is to amuse. The pseudo-context is the last refuge, so to say, of a culture overwhelmed by irrelevance, incoherence, and impotence.

Of course, photography and telegraphy did not strike down at one blow the vast edifice that was typographic culture. The habits of exposition, as I have tried to show, had a long history, and they held powerful sway over the minds of turn-of-the-century Americans. In fact, the early decades of the twentieth century were marked by a great outpouring of brilliant language and literature. In the pages of magazines like the *American Mercury* and *The New Yorker,* in the novels and stories of Faulkner, Fitzgerald, Steinbeck, and Hemingway, and even in the columns of the newspaper giants—the *Herald Tribune,* the *Times*—prose thrilled with a vibrancy and intensity that delighted ear and eye. But this was exposition's nightingale song, most brilliant and sweet as the singer nears the moment of death. It told, for the Age of Exposition, not of new beginnings, but of an end. Beneath its dying melody, a new note had been sounded, and photography and telegraphy set the key. Theirs was a "language" that denied interconnectedness, proceeded without context, argued the irrelevance of history, explained nothing, and offered fascination in place of complexity and coherence. Theirs was a duet of image and instancy, and together they played the tune of a new kind of public discourse in America.

Each of the media that entered the electronic conversation in the late nineteenth and early twentieth centuries followed the lead of the telegraph and the photograph, and amplified their biases. Some, such as film, were by their nature inclined to do so. Others, whose bias was rather toward the amplification of rational speech—like radio—were overwhelmed by the thrust of the new epistemology and came in the end to support it. Together, this ensemble of electronic techniques called into being a new world—a peek-a-boo world, where now this event, now that, pops into view for a moment, then vanishes again. It is a world without much coherence or sense; a world that does not ask us, indeed, does not permit us to do anything; a world that is, like the child's game of peek-a-boo, entirely self-contained. But like peek-a-boo, it is also endlessly entertaining.

Of course, there is nothing wrong with playing peek-a-boo. And there is nothing wrong with entertainment. As some psychiatrist once put it, we all build castles in the air. The problems come when we try to *live* in them. The communications media of the late nineteenth and early twentieth centuries, with telegraphy and photography at their center, called the peek-a-boo world into existence, but we did not come to live there until television. Television gave the epistemological biases of the telegraph and the photograph their most potent expression, raising the interplay of image and instancy to an exquisite and dangerous perfection. And it brought them into the home. We are by now well into a second generation of children for whom television has been their first and most accessible teacher and, for many, their most reliable companion and friend. To put it plainly, television is the command center of the new epistemology. There is no audience so young that it is barred from television. There is no poverty so abject that it must forgo television. There is no education so exalted that it is not modified by television. And most important of all, there is no subject of public interest—politics, news, education, religion, science, sports— that does not find its way to television. Which means that all public understanding of these subjects is shaped by the biases of television.

Television is the command center in subtler ways as well. Our use of other media, for example, is largely orchestrated by television. Through it we learn what telephone system to use, what movies to see, what books, records and magazines to buy, what radio programs to listen to. Television arranges our communications environment for us in ways that no other medium has the power to do.

As a small, ironic example of this point, consider this: In the past few years, we have been learning that the computer is the technology of the future. We are told that our children will fail in school and be left behind in life if they are not "computer literate." We are told that we cannot run our businesses, or compile our shopping lists, or keep our checkbooks tidy unless we own a computer. Perhaps some of this is true. But the most important fact about computers and what they mean to our lives is that we learn about all of this from television. Television has achieved the status of "meta-medium"—an instrument that directs not only our knowledge of the world, but our knowledge of *ways of knowing* as well.

At the same time, television has achieved the status of "myth," as Roland Barthes uses the word. He means by myth a way of understanding the world that is not problematic, that we are not fully conscious of, that seems, in a word, natural. A myth is a way of thinking so deeply embedded in our consciousness that it is invisible. This is now the way of television. We are no longer fascinated or perplexed by its machinery. We do not tell stories of its wonders. We do not confine our television sets to special rooms. We do not doubt the reality of what we see on television, are largely unaware of the special angle of vision it affords. Even the question of how television affects us has receded into the background. The question itself may strike some of us as strange, as if one were to ask how having ears and eyes affects us. Twenty years ago, the question, Does television shape culture or merely reflect it? held considerable interest for many scholars and social critics. The question has largely disappeared as television has gradually *become* our culture. This means, among other things, that we rarely talk about television, only about what is *on* television—that is, about its content. Its ecology, which includes not only its physical characteristics and symbolic code but the conditions in which we normally attend to it, is taken for granted, accepted as natural.

Television has become, so to speak, the background radiation of the social and intellectual universe, the all-but-imperceptible residue of the electronic big bang of a century past, so familiar and so thoroughly integrated with American culture that we no longer hear its faint hissing in the background or see the flickering gray light. This, in turn, means that its epistemology goes largely unnoticed. And the peek-a-boo world it has constructed around us no longer seems even strange.

There is no more disturbing consequence of the electronic and graphic revolution than this: that the world as given to us through television seems natural, not bizarre. For the loss of the sense of the strange is a sign of adjustment, and the extent to which we have adjusted is a measure of the extent to which we have been changed. Our culture's adjustment to the epistemology of television is by now all but complete; we have so thoroughly accepted its definitions of truth, knowledge, and reality that irrelevance seems to us to be filled with import, and incoherence seems eminently sane. And if some of our institutions seem not to fit the template of the times, why it is they, and not the template, that seem to us disordered and strange.

It is my object in the rest of this book to make the epistemology of television visible again. I will try to demonstrate by concrete example that television's way of knowing is uncompromisingly hostile to typography's way of knowing; that television's conversations promote incoherence and triviality; that the phrase "serious television" is a contradiction in terms; and that television speaks in only one persistent voice—the voice of entertainment. Beyond that, I will try to demonstrate that to enter the great television conversation, one American cultural institution after another is learning to speak its terms. Television, in other words, is transforming our culture into one vast arena for show business. It is entirely possible, of course, that in the end we shall find that delightful, and decide we like it just fine. That is exactly what Aldous Huxley feared was coming, fifty years ago.

Part II.

6.

The Age of
Show Business

A dedicated graduate student I know returned to his small apartment the night before a major examination only to discover that his solitary lamp was broken beyond repair. After a whiff of panic, he was able to restore both his equanimity and his chances for a satisfactory grade by turning on the television set, turning off the sound, and with his back to the set, using its light to read important passages on which he was to be tested. This is one use of television—as a source of illuminating the printed page.

But the television screen is more than a light source. It is also a smooth, nearly flat surface on which the printed word may be displayed. We have all stayed at hotels in which the TV set has had a special channel for describing the day's events in letters rolled endlessly across the screen. This is another use of television—as an electronic bulletin board.

Many television sets are also large and sturdy enough to bear the weight of a small library. The top of an old-fashioned RCA console can handle as many as thirty books, and I know one woman who has securely placed her entire collection of Dickens, Flaubert, and Turgenev on the top of a 21-inch Westinghouse. Here is still another use of television—as bookcase.

I bring forward these quixotic uses of television to ridicule the hope harbored by some that television can be used to support the literate tradition. Such a hope represents exactly what Marshall McLuhan used to call "rear-view mirror" thinking: the assumption that a new medium is merely an extension or amplification of an older one; that an automobile, for example, is only a fast horse, or an electric light a powerful candle. To make such a mistake in the matter at hand is to misconstrue entirely how television redefines the meaning of public discourse. Television does not extend or amplify literate culture. It attacks it. If television is a continuation of anything, it is of a tradition begun by the telegraph and photograph in the mid-nineteenth century, not by the printing press in the fifteenth.

What is television? What kinds of conversations does it permit? What are the intellectual tendencies it encourages? What sort of culture does it produce?

These are the questions to be addressed in the rest of this book, and to approach them with a minimum of confusion, I must begin by making a distinction between a technology and a medium. We might say that a technology is to a medium as the brain is to the mind. Like the brain, a technology is a physical apparatus. Like the mind, a medium is a use to which a physical apparatus is put. A technology becomes a medium as it employs a particular symbolic code, as it finds its place in a particular social setting, as it insinuates itself into economic and political contexts. A technology, in other words, is merely a machine. A medium is the social and intellectual environment a machine creates.

Of course, like the brain itself, every technology has an inherent bias. It has within its physical form a predisposition toward being used in certain ways and not others. Only those who know nothing of the history of technology believe that a technology is entirely neutral. There is an old joke that mocks that naive belief. Thomas Edison, it goes, would have revealed his discovery of the electric light much sooner than he did except for the fact that every time he turned it on, he held it to his mouth and said, "Hello? Hello?"

Not very likely. Each technology has an agenda of its own. It is, as I have suggested, a metaphor waiting to unfold. The printing press, for example, had a clear bias toward being used as a linguistic medium. It is *conceivable* to use it exclusively for the reproduction of pictures. And, one imagines, the Roman Catholic Church would not have objected to its being so used in the sixteenth century. Had that been the case, the Protestant Reformation might not have occurred, for as Luther contended, with the word of God on every family's kitchen table, Christians do not require the Papacy to interpret it for them. But in fact there never was much chance that the press would be used solely, or even very much, for the duplication of icons. From its beginning in the fifteenth century, the press was perceived as an extraordinary opportunity for the display and mass distribution of written language. Everything about its technical possibilities led in that direction. One might even say it was invented for that purpose.

The technology of television has a bias, as well. It is conceivable to use television as a lamp, a surface for texts, a bookcase, even as radio. But it has not been so used and will not be so used, at least in America. Thus, in answering the question, What is television?, we must understand as a first point that we are not talking about television as a technology but television as a medium. There are many places in the world where television, though the same technology as it is in America, is an entirely different medium from that which we know. I refer to places where the majority of people do not have television sets, and those who do have only one; where only one station is available; where television does not operate around the clock; where most programs have as their purpose the direct furtherance of government ideology and policy; where commercials are unknown, and "talking heads" are the principal image; where television is mostly used as if it were radio. For these reasons and more television will not have the same meaning or power as it does in America, which is to say, it is possible for a technology to be so used that its potentialities are prevented from developing and its social consequences kept to a minimum.

But in America, this has not been the case. Television has found in liberal democracy and a relatively free market economy a nurturing climate in which its full potentialities as a technology of images could be exploited. One result of this has been that American television programs are in demand all over the world. The total estimate of U.S. television program exports is approximately 100,000 to 200,000 hours, equally divided among Latin America, Asia and Europe.[1] Over the years, programs like "Gunsmoke," "Bonanza," "Mission: Impossible," "Star Trek," "Kojak," and more recently, "Dallas" and "Dynasty" have been as popular in England, Japan, Israel and Norway as in Omaha, Nebraska. I have heard (but not verified) that some years ago the Lapps postponed for several days their annual and, one supposes, essential migratory journey so that they could find out who shot J.R. All of this has occurred simultaneously with the decline of America's moral and political prestige, worldwide. American television programs are in demand not because America is loved but because American television is loved.

We need not be detained too long in figuring out why. In watching American television, one is reminded of George Bernard Shaw's remark on his first seeing the glittering neon signs of Broadway and 42nd Street at night. It must be beautiful, he said, if you cannot read. American television is, indeed, a beautiful spectacle, a visual delight, pouring forth thousands of images on any given day. The average length of a shot on network television is only 3.5 seconds, so that the eye never rests, always has something new to see. Moreover, television offers viewers a variety of subject matter, requires minimal skills to comprehend it, and is largely aimed at emotional gratification. Even commercials, which some regard as an annoyance, are exquisitely crafted, always pleasing to the eye and accompanied by exciting music. There is no question but that the best photography in the world is presently seen on television commercials. American television, in other words, is devoted entirely to supplying its audience with entertainment.

Of course, to say that television is entertaining is merely banal. Such a fact is hardly threatening to a culture, not even worth writing a book about. It may even be a reason for rejoicing. Life, as we like to say, is not a highway strewn with flowers. The sight of a few blossoms here and there may make our journey a trifle more endurable. The Lapps undoubtedly thought so. We may surmise that the ninety million Americans who watch television every night also think so. But what I am claiming here is not that television is entertaining but that it has made entertainment itself the natural format for the representation of all experience. Our television set keeps us in constant communion with the world, but it does so with a face whose smiling countenance is unalterable. The problem is not that television presents us with entertaining subject matter but that all subject matter is presented as entertaining, which is another issue altogether.

To say it still another way: Entertainment is the supra-ideology of all discourse on television. No matter what is depicted or from what point of view, the overarching presumption is that it is there for our amusement and pleasure. That is why even on news shows which provide us daily with fragments of tragedy and barbarism, we are urged by the newscasters to "join them tomorrow." What for? One would think that several minutes of murder and mayhem would suffice as material for a month of sleepless nights. We accept the newscasters' invitation because we know that the "news" is not to be taken seriously, that it is all in fun, so to say. Everything about a news show tells us this—the good looks and amiability of the cast, their pleasant banter, the exciting music that opens and closes the show, the vivid film footage, the attractive commercials—all these and more suggest that what we have just seen is no cause for weeping. A news show, to put it plainly, is a format for entertainment, not for education, reflection or catharsis. And we must not judge too harshly those who have framed it in this way. They are not assembling the news to be read, or broadcasting it to be heard. They are televising the news to be seen. They must follow where their medium leads. There is no conspiracy here, no lack of intelligence, only a straightforward recognition that "good television" has little to do with what is "good" about exposition or other forms of verbal communication but everything to do with what the pictorial images look like.

I should like to illustrate this point by offering the case of the eighty-minute discussion provided by the ABC network on November 20, 1983, following its controversial movie *The Day After*. Though the memory of this telecast has receded for most, I choose this case because, clearly, here was television taking its most "serious" and "responsible" stance. Everything that made up this broadcast recommended it as a critical test of television's capacity to depart from an entertainment mode and rise to the level of public instruction. In the first place, the subject was the possibility of a nuclear holocaust. Second, the film itself had been attacked by several influential bodies politic, including the Reverend Jerry Falwell's Moral Majority. Thus, it was important that the network display television's value and serious intentions as a medium of information and coherent discourse. Third, on the program itself no musical theme was used as background—a significant point since almost all television programs are embedded in music, which helps to tell the audience what emotions are to be called forth. This is a standard theatrical device, and its absence on television is always ominous. Fourth, there were no commercials during the discussion, thus elevating the tone of the event to the state of reverence usually reserved for the funerals of assassinated Presidents. And finally, the participants included Henry Kissinger, Robert McNamara, and Elie Wiesel, each of whom is a symbol of sorts of serious discourse. Although Kissinger, somewhat later, made an appearance on the hit show "Dynasty," he was then and still is a paradigm of intellectual sobriety; and Wiesel, practically a walking metaphor of social conscience. Indeed, the other members of the cast—Carl Sagan, William Buckley and General Brent Scowcroft—are, each in his way, men of intellectual bearing who are not expected to participate in trivial public matters.

The program began with Ted Koppel, master of ceremonies, so to speak, indicating that what followed was not intended to be a debate but a *discussion*. And so those who are interested in philosophies of discourse had an excellent opportunity to observe what serious television means by the word "discussion." Here is what it means: Each of six men was given approximately five minutes to say something about the subject. There was, however, no agreement on exactly what the subject was, and no one felt obliged to respond to anything anyone else said. In fact, it would have been difficult to do so, since the participants were called upon seriatim, as if they were finalists in a beauty contest, each being given his share of minutes in front of the camera. Thus, if Mr. Wiesel, who was called upon last, had a response to Mr. Buckley, who was called upon first, there would have been four commentaries in between, occupying about twenty minutes, so that the audience (if not Mr. Wiesel himself) would have had difficulty remembering the argument which prompted his response. In fact, the participants—most of whom were no strangers to television—largely avoided addressing each other's points. They used their initial minutes and then their subsequent ones to intimate their position or give an impression. Dr. Kissinger, for example, seemed intent on making viewers feel sorry that he was no longer their Secretary of State by reminding everyone of books he had once written, proposals he had once made, and negotiations he had once conducted. Mr. McNamara informed the audience that he had eaten lunch in Germany that very afternoon, and went on to say that he had at least fifteen proposals to reduce nuclear arms. One would have thought that the discussion would turn on this issue, but the others seemed about as interested in it as they were in what he had for lunch in Germany. (Later, he took the initiative to mention three of his proposals but they were not discussed.) Elie Wiesel, in a series of quasi-parables and paradoxes, stressed the tragic nature of the human condition, but because he did not have the time to provide a context for his remarks, he seemed quixotic and confused, conveying an impression of an itinerant rabbi who has wandered into a coven of Gentiles.

In other words, this was no discussion as we normally use the word. Even when the "discussion" period began, there were no arguments or counterarguments, no scrutiny of assumptions, no explanations, no elaborations, no definitions. Carl Sagan made, in my opinion, the most coherent statement—a four-minute rationale for a nuclear freeze—but it contained at least two questionable assumptions and was not carefully examined. Apparently, no one wanted to take time from his own few minutes to call attention to someone else's. Mr. Koppel, for his part, felt obliged to keep the "show" moving, and though he occasionally pursued what he discerned as a line of thought, he was more concerned to give each man his fair allotment of time.

But it is not time constraints alone that produce such fragmented and discontinuous language. When a television show is in process, it is very nearly impermissible to say, "Let me think about that" or "I don't know" or "What do you mean when you say . . . ?" or "From what sources does your information come?" This type of discourse not only slows down the tempo of the show but creates the impression of uncertainty or lack of finish. It tends to reveal people in the *act of thinking*, which is as disconcerting and boring on television as it is on a Las Vegas stage. Thinking does not play well on television, a fact that television directors discovered long ago. There is not much to *see* in it. It is, in a phrase, not a performing art. But television demands a performing art, and so what the ABC network gave us was a picture of men of sophisticated verbal skills and political understanding being brought to heel by a medium that requires them to fashion performances rather than ideas. Which accounts for why the eighty minutes were very entertaining, in the way of a Samuel Beckett play: The intimations of gravity hung heavy, the meaning passeth all understanding. The performances, of course, were highly professional. Sagan abjured the turtle-neck sweater in which he starred when he did "Cosmos." He even had his hair cut for the event. His part was that of the logical scientist speaking in behalf of the planet. It is to be doubted that Paul Newman could have done better in the role, although Leonard Nimoy might have. Scowcroft was suitably military in his bearing—terse and distant, the unbreakable defender of national security. Kissinger, as always, was superb in the part of the knowing world statesman, weary of the sheer responsibility of keeping disaster at bay. Koppel played to perfection the part of a moderator, pretending, as it were, that he was sorting out ideas while, in fact, he was merely directing the performances. At the end, one could only applaud those performances, which is what a good television program always aims to achieve; that is to say, applause, not reflection.

I do not say categorically that it is impossible to use television as a carrier of coherent language or thought in process. William Buckley's own program, "Firing Line," occasionally shows people in the act of thinking but who also happen to have television cameras pointed at them. There are other programs, such as "Meet the Press" or "The Open Mind," which clearly strive to maintain a sense of intellectual decorum and typographic tradition, but they are scheduled so that they do not compete with programs of great visual interest, since otherwise, they will not be watched. After all, it is not unheard of that a format will occasionally go against the bias of its medium. For example, the most popular radio program of the early 1940's featured a ventriloquist, and in those days, I heard more than once the feet of a tap dancer on the "Major Bowes' Amateur Hour." (Indeed, if I am not mistaken, he even once featured a pantomimist.) But ventriloquism, dancing and mime do not play well on radio, just as sustained, complex talk does not play well on television. It can be made to play tolerably well if only one camera is used and the visual image is kept constant—as when the President gives a speech. But this is not television at its best, and it is not television that most people will choose to watch. The single most important fact about television is that people *watch* it, which is why it is called "tele*vision.*" And what they watch, and like to watch, are moving pictures—millions of them, of short duration and dynamic variety. It is in the nature of the medium that it must suppress the content of ideas in order to accommodate the requirements of visual interest; that is to say, to accommodate the values of show business.

Film, records and radio (now that it is an adjunct of the music industry) are, of course, equally devoted to entertaining the culture, and their effects in altering the style of American discourse are not insignificant. But television is different because it encompasses all forms of discourse. No one goes to a movie to find out about government policy or the latest scientific advances. No one buys a record to find out the baseball scores or the weather or the latest murder. No one turns on radio anymore for soap operas or a presidential address (if a television set is at hand). But everyone goes to television for all these things and more, which is why television resonates so powerfully throughout the culture. Television is our culture's principal mode of knowing about itself. Therefore—and this is the critical point—how television stages the world becomes the model for how the world is properly to be staged. It is not merely that on the television screen entertainment is the metaphor for all discourse. It is that off the screen the same metaphor prevails. As typography once dictated the style of conducting politics, religion, business, education, law and other important social matters, television now takes command. In courtrooms, classrooms, operating rooms, board rooms, churches and even airplanes, Americans no longer talk to each other, they entertain each other. They do not exchange ideas; they exchange images. They do not argue with propositions; they argue with good looks, celebrities and commercials. For the message of television as metaphor is not only that all the world is a stage but that the stage is located in Las Vegas, Nevada.

In Chicago, for example, the Reverend Greg Sakowicz, a Roman Catholic priest, mixes his religious teaching with rock 'n' roll music. According to the Associated Press, the Reverend Sakowicz is both an associate pastor at the Church of the Holy Spirit in Schaumberg (a suburb of Chicago) and a disc jockey at WKQX. On his show, "The Journey Inward," Father Sakowicz chats in soft tones about such topics as family relationships or commitment, and interposes his sermons with "the sound of *Billboard*'s Top 10." He says that his preaching is not done "in a churchy way," and adds, "You don't have to be boring in order to be holy."

Meanwhile in New York City at St. Patrick's Cathedral, Father John J. O'Connor put on a New York Yankee baseball cap as he mugged his way through his installation as Archbishop of the New York Archdiocese. He got off some excellent gags, at least one of which was specifically directed at Mayor Edward Koch, who was a member of his audience; that is to say, he was a congregant. At his next public performance, the new archbishop donned a New York Mets baseball cap. These events were, of course, televised, and were vastly entertaining, largely because Archbishop (now Cardinal) O'Connor has gone Father Sakowicz one better: Whereas the latter believes that you don't have to be boring to be holy, the former apparently believes you don't have to be holy at all.

In Phoenix, Arizona, Dr. Edward Dietrich performed triple bypass surgery on Bernard Schuler. The operation was successful, which was nice for Mr. Schuler. It was also on television, which was nice for America. The operation was carried by at least fifty television stations in the United States, and also by the British Broadcasting Corporation. A two-man panel of narrators (a play-by-play and color man, so to speak) kept viewers informed about what they were seeing. It was not clear as to why this event was televised, but it resulted in transforming both Dr. Dietrich and Mr. Schuler's chest into celebrities. Perhaps because he has seen too many doctor shows on television, Mr. Schuler was uncommonly confident about the outcome of his surgery. "There is no way in hell they are going to lose me on live TV," he said.[2]

As reported with great enthusiasm by both WCBS-TV and WNBC-TV in 1984, the Philadelphia public schools have embarked on an experiment in which children will have their curriculum sung to them. Wearing Walkman equipment, students were shown listening to rock music whose lyrics were about the eight parts of speech. Mr. Jocko Henderson, who thought of this idea, is planning to delight students further by subjecting mathematics and history, as well as English, to the rigors of a rock music format. In fact, this is not Mr. Henderson's idea at all. It was pioneered by the Children's Television Workshop, whose television show "Sesame Street" is an expensive illustration of the idea that education is indistinguishable from entertainment. Nonetheless, Mr. Henderson has a point in his favor. Whereas "Sesame Street" merely attempts to make learning to read a form of light entertainment, the Philadelphia experiment aims to make the classroom itself into a rock concert.

In New Bedford, Massachusetts, a rape trial was televised, to the delight of audiences who could barely tell the difference between the trial and their favorite mid-day soap opera. In Florida, trials of varying degrees of seriousness, including murder, are regularly televised and are considered to be more entertaining than most fictional courtroom dramas. All of this is done in the interests of "public education." For the same high purpose, plans are afoot, it is rumored, to televise confessionals. To be called "Secrets of the Confessional Box," the program will, of course, carry the warning that some of its material may be offensive to children and therefore parental guidance is suggested.

On a United Airlines flight from Chicago to Vancouver, a stewardess announces that its passengers will play a game. The passenger with the most credit cards will win a bottle of champagne. A man from Boston with twelve credit cards wins. A second game requires the passengers to guess the collective age of the cabin crew. A man from Chicago guesses 128, and wins another bottle of wine. During the second game, the air turns choppy and the Fasten Seat Belt sign goes on. Very few people notice, least of all the cabin crew, who keep up a steady flow of gags on the intercom. When the plane reaches its destination, everyone seems to agree that it's fun to fly from Chicago to Vancouver.

On February 7, 1985, *The New York Times* reported that Professor Charles Pine of Rutgers University (Newark campus) was named Professor of the Year by the Council for the Support and Advancement of Education. In explaining why he has such a great impact on his students, Professor Pine said: "I have some gimmicks I use all the time. If you reach the end of the blackboard, I keep writing on the wall. It always gets a laugh. The way I show what a glass molecule does is to run over to one wall and bounce off it, and run over to the other wall." His students are, perhaps, too young to recall that James Cagney used this "molecule move" to great effect in *Yankee Doodle Dandy*. If I am not mistaken, Donald O'Connor duplicated it in *Singin' in the Rain*. So far as I know, it has been used only once before in a classroom: Hegel tried it several times in demonstrating how the dialectical method works.

The Pennsylvania Amish try to live in isolation from mainstream American culture. Among other things, their religion opposes the veneration of graven images, which means that the Amish are forbidden to see movies or to be photographed. But apparently their religion has not got around to disallowing seeing movies *when* they are being photographed. In the summer of 1984, for example, a Paramount Pictures crew descended upon Lancaster County to film the movie *Witness*, which is about a detective, played by Harrison Ford, who falls in love with an Amish woman. Although the Amish were warned by their church not to interfere with the film makers, it turned out that some Amish welders ran to see the action as soon as their work was done. Other devouts lay in the grass some distance away, and looked down on the set with binoculars. "We read about the movie in the paper," said an Amish woman. "The kids even cut out Harrison Ford's picture." She added: "But it doesn't really matter that much to them. Somebody told us he was in *Star Wars* but that doesn't mean anything to us." [3] The last time a similar conclusion was drawn was when the executive director of the American Association of Blacksmiths remarked that he had read about the automobile but that he was convinced it would have no consequences for the future of his organization.

In the Winter, 1984, issue of the *Official Video Journal* there appears a full-page advertisement for "The Genesis Project." The project aims to convert the Bible into a series of movies. The end-product, to be called "The New Media Bible," will consist of 225 hours of film and will cost a quarter of a billion dollars. Producer John Heyman, whose credits include *Saturday Night Fever* and *Grease*, is one of the film makers most committed to the project. "Simply stated," he is quoted as saying, "I got hooked on the Bible." The famous Israeli actor Topol, best known for his role as Tevye in *Fiddler on the Roof*, will play the role of Abraham. The advertisement does not say who will star as God but, given the producer's background, there is some concern that it might be John Travolta.

At the commencement exercises at Yale University in 1983, several honorary degrees were awarded, including one to Mother Teresa. As she and other humanitarians and scholars, each in turn, received their awards, the audience applauded appropriately but with a slight hint of reserve and impatience, for it wished to give its heart to the final recipient who waited shyly in the wings. As the details of her achievements were being recounted, many people left their seats and surged toward the stage to be closer to the great woman. And when the name Meryl Streep was announced, the audience unleashed a sonic boom of affection to wake the New Haven dead. One man who was present when Bob Hope received his honorary doctorate at another institution said that Dr. Streep's applause surpassed Dr. Hope's. Knowing how to please a crowd as well as anyone, the intellectual leaders at Yale invited Dick Cavett, the talk-show host, to deliver the commencement address the following year. It is rumored that this year, Don Rickles will receive a Doctorate of Humane Letters and Lola Falana will give the commencement address.

Prior to the 1984 presidential elections, the two candidates confronted each other on television in what were called "debates." These events were not in the least like the Lincoln-Douglas debates or anything else that goes by the name. Each candidate was given five minutes to address such questions as, What is (or would be) your policy in Central America? His opposite number was then given one minute for a rebuttal. In such circumstances, complexity, documentation and logic can play no role, and, indeed, on several occasions syntax itself was abandoned entirely. It is no matter. The men were less concerned with giving arguments than with "giving off" impressions, which is what television does best. Post-debate commentary largely avoided any evaluation of the candidates' ideas, since there were none to evaluate. Instead, the debates were conceived as boxing matches, the relevant question being, Who KO'd whom? The answer was determined by the "style" of the men—how they looked, fixed their gaze, smiled, and delivered one-liners. In the second debate, President Reagan got off a swell one-liner when asked a question about his age. The following day, several newspapers indicated that Ron had KO'd Fritz with his joke. Thus, the leader of the free world is chosen by the people in the Age of Television.

What all of this means is that our culture has moved toward a new way of conducting its business, especially its important business. The nature of its discourse is changing as the demarcation line between what is show business and what is not becomes harder to see with each passing day. Our priests and presidents, our surgeons and lawyers, our educators and newscasters need worry less about satisfying the demands of their discipline than the demands of good showmanship. Had Irving Berlin changed one word in the title of his celebrated song, he would have been as prophetic, albeit more terse, as Aldous Huxley. He need only have written, There's No Business But Show Business.

7.

"Now . . . This"

The American humorist H. Allen Smith once suggested that of all the worrisome words in the English language, the scariest is "uh oh," as when a physician looks at your X-rays, and with knitted brow says, "Uh oh." I should like to suggest that the words which are the title of this chapter are as ominous as any, all the more so because they are spoken without knitted brow—indeed, with a kind of idiot's delight. The phrase, if that's what it may be called, adds to our grammar a new part of speech, a conjunction that does not connect anything to anything but does the opposite: separates everything from everything. As such, it serves as a compact metaphor for the discontinuities in so much that passes for public discourse in present-day America.

"Now . . . this" is commonly used on radio and television newscasts to indicate that what one has just heard or seen has no relevance to what one is about to hear or see, or possibly to anything one is ever likely to hear or see. The phrase is a means of acknowledging the fact that the world as mapped by the speeded-up electronic media has no order or meaning and is not to be taken seriously. There is no murder so brutal, no earthquake so devastating, no political blunder so costly—for that matter, no ball score so tantalizing or weather report so threatening—that it cannot be erased from our minds by a newscaster saying, "Now . . . this." The newscaster means that you have thought long enough on the previous matter (approximately forty-five seconds), that you must not be morbidly preoccupied with it (let us say, for ninety seconds), and that you must now give your attention to another fragment of news or a commercial.

Television did not invent the "Now . . . this" world view. As I have tried to show, it is the offspring of the intercourse between telegraphy and photography. But it is through television that it has been nurtured and brought to a perverse maturity. For on television, nearly every half hour is a discrete event, separated in content, context, and emotional texture from what precedes and follows it. In part because television sells its time in seconds and minutes, in part because television must use images rather than words, in part because its audience can move freely to and from the television set, programs are structured so that almost each eight-minute segment may stand as a complete event in itself. Viewers are rarely required to carry over any thought or feeling from one parcel of time to another.

Of course, in television's presentation of the "news of the day," we may see the "Now . . . this" mode of discourse in its boldest and most embarrassing form. For there, we are presented not only with fragmented news but news without context, without consequences, without value, and therefore without essential seriousness; that is to say, news as pure entertainment.

Consider, for example, how you would proceed if you were given the opportunity to produce a television news show for any station concerned to attract the largest possible audience. You would, first, choose a cast of players, each of whom has a face that is both "likable" and "credible." Those who apply would, in fact, submit to you their eight-by-ten glossies, from which you would eliminate those whose countenances are not suitable for nightly display. This means that you will exclude women who are not beautiful or who are over the age of fifty, men who are bald, all people who are overweight or whose noses are too long or whose eyes are too close together. You will try, in other words, to assemble a cast of talking hair-do's.

At the very least, you will want those whose faces would not be unwelcome on a magazine cover.

Christine Craft has just such a face, and so she applied for a co-anchor position on KMBC-TV in Kansas City. According to a lawyer who represented her in a sexism suit she later brought against the station, the management of KMBC-TV "loved Christine's look." She was accordingly hired in January 1981. She was fired in August 1981 because research indicated that her appearance "hampered viewer acceptance." [1] What exactly does "hampered viewer acceptance" mean? And what does it have to do with the news? Hampered viewer acceptance means the same thing for television news as it does for any television show: Viewers do not like looking at the performer. It also means that viewers do not believe the performer, that she lacks credibility. In the case of a theatrical performance, we have a sense of what that implies: The actor does not persuade the audience that he or she is the character being portrayed. But what does lack of credibility imply in the case of a news show? What character is a co-anchor playing? And how do we decide that the performance lacks verisimilitude? Does the audience believe that the newscaster is lying, that what is reported did not in fact happen, that something important is being concealed?

It is frightening to think that this may be so, that the perception of the truth of a report rests heavily on the acceptability of the newscaster. In the ancient world, there was a tradition of banishing or killing the bearer of bad tidings. Does the television news show restore, in a curious form, this tradition? Do we banish those who tell us the news when we do not care for the face of the teller? Does television countermand the warnings we once received about the fallacy of the ad hominem argument?

If the answer to any of these questions is even a qualified "Yes," then here is an issue worthy of the attention of epistemologists. Stated in its simplest form, it is that television provides a new (or, possibly, restores an old) definition of truth:

The credibility of the teller is the ultimate test of the truth of a proposition. ''Credibility'' here does not refer to the past record of the teller for making statements that have survived the rigors of reality-testing. It refers only to the impression of sincerity, authenticity, vulnerability or attractiveness (choose one or more) conveyed by the actor/reporter.

This is a matter of considerable importance, for it goes beyond the question of how truth is perceived on television news shows. If on television, credibility replaces reality as the decisive test of truth-telling, political leaders need not trouble themselves very much with reality provided that their performances consistently generate a sense of verisimilitude. I suspect, for example, that the dishonor that now shrouds Richard Nixon results not from the fact that he lied but that on television he looked like a liar. Which, if true, should bring no comfort to anyone, not even veteran Nixon-haters. For the alternative possibilities are that one may look like a liar but be telling the truth; or even worse, look like a truth-teller but in fact be lying.

As a producer of a television news show, you would be well aware of these matters and would be careful to choose your cast on the basis of criteria used by David Merrick and other successful impresarios. Like them, you would then turn your attention to staging the show on principles that maximize entertainment value. You would, for example, select a musical theme for the show. All television news programs begin, end, and are somewhere in between punctuated with music. I have found very few Americans who regard this custom as peculiar, which fact I have taken as evidence for the dissolution of lines of demarcation between serious public discourse and entertainment. What has music to do with the news? Why is it there? It is there, I assume, for the same reason music is used in the theater and films—to create a mood and provide a leitmotif for the entertainment. If there were no music—as is the case when any television program is interrupted for a news flash—viewers would expect something truly alarming, possibly life-altering.

But as long as the music is there as a frame for the program, the viewer is comforted to believe that there is nothing to be greatly alarmed about; that, in fact, the events that are reported have as much relation to reality as do scenes in a play.

This perception of a news show as a stylized dramatic performance whose content has been staged largely to entertain is reinforced by several other features, including the fact that the average length of any story is forty-five seconds. While brevity does not always suggest triviality, in this case it clearly does. It is simply not possible to convey a sense of seriousness about any event if its implications are exhausted in less than one minute's time. In fact, it is quite obvious that TV news has no intention of suggesting that any story *has* any implications, for that would require viewers to continue to think about it when it is done and therefore obstruct their attending to the next story that waits panting in the wings. In any case, viewers are not provided with much opportunity to be distracted from the next story since in all likelihood it will consist of some film footage. Pictures have little difficulty in overwhelming words, and short-circuiting introspection. As a television producer, you would be certain to give both prominence and precedence to any event for which there is some sort of visual documentation. A suspected killer being brought into a police station, the angry face of a cheated consumer, a barrel going over Niagara Falls (with a person alleged to be in it), the President disembarking from a helicopter on the White House lawn—these are always fascinating or amusing, and easily satisfy the requirements of an entertaining show. It is, of course, not necessary that the visuals actually document the point of a story. Neither is it necessary to explain why such images are intruding themselves on public consciousness. Film footage justifies itself, as every television producer well knows.

It is also of considerable help in maintaining a high level of unreality that the newscasters do not pause to grimace or shiver when they speak their prefaces or epilogs to the film clips. Indeed, many newscasters do not appear to grasp the meaning of what they are saying, and some hold to a fixed and ingratiating enthusiasm as they report on earthquakes, mass killings and other disasters. Viewers would be quite disconcerted by any show of concern or terror on the part of newscasters. Viewers, after all, are partners with the newscasters in the "Now . . . this" culture, and they expect the newscaster to play out his or her role as a character who is marginally serious but who stays well clear of authentic understanding. The viewers, for their part, will not be caught contaminating their responses with a sense of reality, any more than an audience at a play would go scurrying to call home because a character on stage has said that a murderer is loose in the neighborhood.

The viewers also know that no matter how grave any fragment of news may appear (for example, on the day I write a Marine Corps general has declared that nuclear war between the United States and Russia is inevitable), it will shortly be followed by a series of commercials that will, in an instant, defuse the import of the news, in fact render it largely banal. This is a key element in the structure of a news program and all by itself refutes any claim that television news is designed as a serious form of public discourse. Imagine what you would think of me, and this book, if I were to pause here, tell you that I will return to my discussion in a moment, and then proceed to write a few words in behalf of United Airlines or the Chase Manhattan Bank. You would rightly think that I had no respect for you and, certainly, no respect for the subject. And if I did this not once but several times in each chapter, you would think the whole enterprise unworthy of your attention. Why, then, do we not think a news show similarly unworthy? The reason, I believe, is that whereas we expect books and even other media (such as film) to maintain a consistency of tone and a continuity of content, we have no such expectation of television, and especially television news. We have become so accustomed to its discontinuities that we are no longer struck dumb, as any sane person would be, by a newscaster who having just reported that a nuclear war is inevitable goes on to say that he will be right back after this word from Burger King; who says, in other words, "Now . . . this." One can hardly overestimate the damage that such juxtapositions do to our sense of the world as a serious place. The damage is especially massive to youthful viewers who depend so much on television for their clues as to how to respond to the world. In watching television news, they, more than any other segment of the audience, are drawn into an epistemology based on the assumption that all reports of cruelty and death are greatly exaggerated and, in any case, not to be taken seriously or responded to sanely.

I should go so far as to say that embedded in the surrealistic frame of a television news show is a theory of anticommunication, featuring a type of discourse that abandons logic, reason, sequence and rules of contradiction. In aesthetics, I believe the name given to this theory is Dadaism; in philosophy, nihilism; in psychiatry, schizophrenia. In the parlance of the theater, it is known as vaudeville.

For those who think I am here guilty of hyperbole, I offer the following description of television news by Robert MacNeil, executive editor and co-anchor of the "MacNeil-Lehrer Newshour." The idea, he writes, "is to keep everything brief, not to strain the attention of anyone but instead to provide constant stimulation through variety, novelty, action, and movement. You are required . . . to pay attention to no concept, no character, and no problem for more than a few seconds at a time." [2] He goes on to say that the assumptions controlling a news show are "that bite-sized is best, that complexity must be avoided, that nuances are dispensable, that qualifications impede the simple message, that visual stimulation is a substitute for thought, and that verbal precision is an anachronism." [3]

Robert MacNeil has more reason than most to give testimony about the television news show as vaudeville act. The "MacNeil-Lehrer Newshour" is an unusual and gracious attempt to bring to television some of the elements of typographic discourse. The program abjures visual stimulation, consists largely of extended explanations of events and in-depth interviews (which even there means only five to ten minutes), limits the number of stories covered, and emphasizes background and coherence. But television has exacted its price for MacNeil's rejection of a show business format. By television's standards, the audience is minuscule, the program is confined to public-television stations, and it is a good guess that the combined salary of MacNeil and Lehrer is one-fifth of Dan Rather's or Tom Brokaw's.

If you were a producer of a television news show for a commercial station, you would not have the option of defying television's requirements. It would be demanded of you that you strive for the largest possible audience, and, as a consequence and in spite of your best intentions, you would arrive at a production very nearly resembling MacNeil's description. Moreover, you would include some things MacNeil does not mention. You would try to make celebrities of your newscasters. You would advertise the show, both in the press and on television itself. You would do "news briefs," to serve as an inducement to viewers. You would have a weatherman as comic relief, and a sportscaster whose language is a touch uncouth (as a way of his relating to the beer-drinking common man). You would, in short, package the whole event as any producer might who is in the entertainment business.

The result of all this is that Americans are the best entertained and quite likely the least well-informed people in the Western world. I say this in the face of the popular conceit that television, as a window to the world, has made Americans exceedingly well informed. Much depends here, of course, on what is meant by being informed. I will pass over the now tiresome polls that tell us that, at any given moment, 70 percent of our citizens do not know who is the Secretary of State or the Chief Justice of the Supreme Court. Let us consider, instead, the case of Iran during the drama that was called the ''Iranian Hostage Crisis.'' I don't suppose there has been a story in years that received more continuous attention from television. We may assume, then, that Americans know most of what there is to know about this unhappy event. And now, I put these questions to you: Would it be an exaggeration to say that not one American in a hundred knows what language the Iranians speak? Or what the word ''Ayatollah'' means or implies? Or knows any details of the tenets of Iranian religious beliefs? Or the main outlines of their political history? Or knows who the Shah was, and where he came from?

Nonetheless, everyone had an opinion about this event, for in America everyone is entitled to an opinion, and it is certainly useful to have a few when a pollster shows up. But these are opinions of a quite different order from eighteenth- or nineteenth-century opinions. It is probably more accurate to call them emotions rather than opinions, which would account for the fact that they change from week to week, as the pollsters tell us. What is happening here is that television is altering the meaning of ''being informed'' by creating a species of information that might properly be called *disinformation*. I am using this word almost in the precise sense in which it is used by spies in the CIA or KGB. Disinformation does not mean false information. It means misleading information—misplaced, irrelevant, fragmented or superficial information—information that creates the illusion of knowing something but which in fact leads one away from knowing. In saying this, I do not mean to imply that television news deliberately aims to deprive Americans of a coherent, contextual understanding of their world. I mean to say that when news is packaged as entertainment, that is the inevitable result. And in saying that the television news show entertains but does not inform, I am saying something far more serious than that we are being deprived of authentic information. I am saying we are losing our sense of what it means to be

well informed. Ignorance is always correctable. But what shall
we do if we take ignorance to be knowledge?

Here is a startling example of how this process bedevils us. A
New York Times article is headlined on February 15, 1983:

REAGAN MISSTATEMENTS GETTING LESS ATTENTION

The article begins in the following way:

President Reagan's aides used to become visibly alarmed at suggestions that he had given mangled and perhaps misleading accounts of his policies or of current events in general. That doesn't
seem to happen much anymore.

Indeed, the President continues to make debatable assertions of
fact but news accounts do not deal with them as extensively as
they once did. In the view of White House officials, the declining
news coverage mirrors a *decline in interest by the general public.* (my
italics)

This report is not so much a news story as a story about the
news, and our recent history suggests that it is not about Ronald
Reagan's charm. It is about how news is defined, and I believe
the story would be quite astonishing to both civil libertarians
and tyrants of an earlier time. Walter Lippmann, for example,
wrote in 1920: "There can be no liberty for a community which
lacks the means by which to detect lies." For all of his pessi-
mism about the possibilities of restoring an eighteenth- and
nineteenth-century level of public discourse, Lippmann assumed, as did Thomas Jefferson before him, that with a well-
trained press functioning as a lie-detector, the public's interest
in a President's mangling of the truth would be piqued, in both
senses of that word. Given the means to detect lies, he believed,
the public could not be indifferent to their consequences.

But this case refutes his assumption. The reporters who cover
the White House are ready and able to expose lies, and thus

create the grounds for informed and indignant opinion. But apparently the public declines to take an interest. To press reports of White House dissembling, the public has replied with Queen Victoria's famous line: "We are not amused." However, here the words mean something the Queen did not have in mind. They mean that what is not amusing does not compel their attention. Perhaps if the President's lies could be demonstrated by pictures and accompanied by music the public would raise a curious eyebrow. If a movie, like *All the President's Men*, could be made from his misleading accounts of government policy, if there were a break-in of some sort or sinister characters laundering money, attention would quite likely be paid. We do well to remember that President Nixon did not begin to come undone until his lies were given a theatrical setting at the Watergate hearings. But we do not have anything like that here. Apparently, all President Reagan does is *say* things that are not entirely true. And there is nothing entertaining in that.

But there is a subtler point to be made here. Many of the President's "misstatements" fall in the category of contradictions—mutually exclusive assertions that cannot possibly both, in the same context, be true. "In the same context" is the key phrase here, for it is context that defines contradiction. There is no problem in someone's remarking that he prefers oranges to apples, and also remarking that he prefers apples to oranges—not if one statement is made in the context of choosing a wallpaper design and the other in the context of selecting fruit for dessert. In such a case, we have statements that are opposites, but not contradictory. But if the statements are made in a single, continuous, and coherent context, then they are contradictions, and cannot both be true. Contradiction, in short, requires that statements and events be perceived as interrelated aspects of a continuous and coherent context. Disappear the context, or fragment it, and contradiction disappears. This point is nowhere made more clear to me than in conferences with my younger students about their writing. "Look here," I say. "In this paragraph you have said one thing. And in that you have said the opposite. Which is it to be?" They are polite, and wish to please, but they are as baffled by the question as I am by the response. "I know," they will say, "but that is *there* and this is *here.* " The difference between us is that I assume "there" and "here," "now" and "then," one paragraph and the next to be connected, to be continuous, to be part of the same coherent world of thought. That is the way of typographic discourse, and typography is the universe I'm "coming from," as they say. But they are coming from a different universe of discourse altogether: the "Now . . . this" world of television. The fundamental assumption of that world is not coherence but discontinuity. And in a world of discontinuities, contradiction is useless as a test of truth or merit, because contradiction does not exist.

My point is that we are by now so thoroughly adjusted to the "Now . . . this" world of news—a world of fragments, where events stand alone, stripped of any connection to the past, or to the future, or to other events—that all assumptions of coherence have vanished. And so, perforce, has contradiction. In the context of *no context,* so to speak, it simply disappears. And in its absence, what possible interest could there be in a list of what the President says *now* and what he said *then?* It is merely a rehash of old news, and there is nothing interesting or entertaining in that. The only thing to be amused about is the bafflement of reporters at the public's indifference. There is an irony in the fact that the very group that has taken the world apart should, on trying to piece it together again, be surprised that no one notices much, or cares.

For all his perspicacity, George Orwell would have been stymied by this situation; there is nothing "Orwellian" about it. The President does not have the press under his thumb. *The New York Times* and *The Washington Post* are not *Pravda;* the Associated Press is not Tass. And there is no Newspeak here. Lies have not been defined as truth nor truth as lies. All that has happened is that the public has adjusted to incoherence and been amused into indifference. Which is why Aldous Huxley would not in the least be surprised by the story. Indeed, he prophesied its coming. He believed that it is far more likely that the Western democracies will dance and dream themselves into oblivion than march into it, single file and manacled. Huxley grasped, as Orwell did not, that it is not necessary to conceal anything from a public insensible to contradiction and narcoticized by technological diversions. Although Huxley did not specify that television would be our main line to the drug, he would have no difficulty accepting Robert MacNeil's observation that "Television is the *soma* of Aldous Huxley's *Brave New World.*" Big Brother turns out to be Howdy Doody.

I do not mean that the trivialization of public information is all accomplished *on* television. I mean that television is the paradigm for our conception of public information. As the printing press did in an earlier time, television has achieved the power to define the form in which news must come, and it has also defined how we shall respond to it. In presenting news to us packaged as vaudeville, television induces other media to do the same, so that the total information environment begins to mirror television.

For example, America's newest and highly successful national newspaper, *USA Today,* is modeled precisely on the format of television. It is sold on the street in receptacles that look like television sets. Its stories are uncommonly short, its design leans heavily on pictures, charts and other graphics, some of them printed in various colors. Its weather maps are a visual delight; its sports section includes enough pointless statistics to distract a computer. As a consequence, *USA Today,* which began publication in September 1982, has become the third largest daily in the United States (as of July 1984, according to the Audit Bureau of Circulations), moving quickly to overtake the *Daily News* and the *Wall Street Journal.* Journalists of a more traditional bent have criticized it for its superficiality and theatrics, but the paper's editors remain steadfast in their disregard of typographic standards. The paper's Editor-in-Chief, John Quinn, has said: "We are not up to undertaking projects of the dimensions needed to win prizes. They don't give awards for the best investigative paragraph."[4] Here is an astonishing tribute to the resonance of television's epistemology: In the age of television, the paragraph is becoming the basic unit of news in print media. Moreover, Mr. Quinn need not fret too long about being deprived of awards. As other newspapers join in the transformation, the time cannot be far off when awards will be given for the best investigative sentence.

It needs also to be noted here that new and successful magazines such as *People* and *Us* are not only examples of television-oriented print media but have had an extraordinary "ricochet" effect on television itself. Whereas television taught the magazines that news is nothing but entertainment, the magazines have taught television that nothing but entertainment is news. Television programs, such as "Entertainment Tonight," turn information about entertainers and celebrities into "serious" cultural content, so that the circle begins to close: Both the form and content of news become entertainment.

Radio, of course, is the least likely medium to join in the descent into a Huxleyan world of technological narcotics. It is, after all, particularly well suited to the transmission of rational, complex language. Nonetheless, and even if we disregard radio's captivation by the music industry, we appear to be left with the chilling fact that such language as radio allows us to hear is increasingly primitive, fragmented, and largely aimed at invoking visceral response; which is to say, it is the linguistic analogue to the ubiquitous rock music that is radio's principal source of income. As I write, the trend in call-in shows is for the "host" to insult callers whose language does not, in itself, go much beyond humanoid grunting. Such programs have little content, as this word used to be defined, and are merely of archeological interest in that they give us a sense of what a dialogue among Neanderthals might have been like. More to the point, the language of radio newscasts has become, under the influence of television, increasingly decontextualized and discontinuous, so that the possibility of anyone's knowing about the world, as against merely knowing *of* it, is effectively blocked. In New York City, radio station WINS entreats its listeners to "Give us twenty-two minutes and we'll give you the world." This is said without irony, and its audience, we may assume, does not regard the slogan as the conception of a disordered mind.

And so, we move rapidly into an information environment which may rightly be called trivial pursuit. As the game of that name uses facts as a source of amusement, so do our sources of news. It has been demonstrated many times that a culture can survive misinformation and false opinion. It has not yet been demonstrated whether a culture can survive if it takes the measure of the world in twenty-two minutes. Or if the value of its news is determined by the number of laughs it provides.

8.

Shuffle Off
to Bethlehem

There is an evangelical preacher on television who goes by the name of Reverend Terry. She appears to be in her early fifties, and features a coiffure of which it has been said that it cannot be mussed, only broken. Reverend Terry is energetic and folksy, and uses a style of preaching modeled on early Milton Berle. When her audiences are shown in reaction shots, they are almost always laughing. As a consequence, it would be difficult to distinguish them from audiences, say, at the Sands Hotel in Las Vegas, except for the fact that they have a slightly cleaner, more wholesome look. Reverend Terry tries to persuade them, as well as those "at home," to change their ways by finding Jesus Christ. To help her do this, she offers a "prosperity Campaign Kit," which appears to have a dual purpose: As it brings one nearer to Jesus, it also provides advice on how to increase one's bank account. This makes her followers extremely happy and confirms their predisposition to believe that prosperity is the true aim of religion. Perhaps God disagrees. As of this writing, Reverend Terry has been obliged to declare bankruptcy and temporarily halt her ministrations.

Pat Robertson is the master of ceremonies of the highly successful "700 Club," a television show and religious organization of sorts to which you can belong by paying fifteen dollars per month. (Of course, anyone with cable television can watch the show free of charge.) Reverend Robertson does his act in a much lower register than Reverend Terry. He is modest, intelligent, and has the kind of charm television viewers would associate with a cool-headed talk-show host. His appeal to godliness is considerably more sophisticated than Reverend Terry's, at least from the standpoint of television. Indeed, he appears to use as his model of communication "Entertainment Tonight." His program includes interviews, singers and taped segments with entertainers who are born-again Christians. For example, all of the chorus girls in Don Ho's Hawaiian act are born-again, and in one segment, we are shown them both at prayer and on stage (although not at the same time). The program also includes taped reenactments of people who, having been driven to the edge of despair, are saved by the 700 Club. Such people play themselves in these finely crafted docu-dramas. In one, we are shown a woman racked with anxiety. She cannot concentrate on her wifely duties. The television shows and movies she sees induce a generalized fear of the world. Paranoia closes in. She even begins to believe that her own children are trying to kill her. As the play proceeds, we see her in front of her television set chancing upon the 700 Club. She becomes interested in its message. She allows Jesus to enter her heart. She is saved. At the end of the play, we see her going about her business, calmly and cheerfully, her eyes illuminated with peace. And so, we may say that the 700 Club has twice elevated her to a state of transcendence: first, by putting her in the presence of Jesus; second, by making her into a television star. To the uninitiated, it is not entirely clear which is the higher estate.

Toward the end of each 700 Club show, the following day's acts are announced. They are many and various. The program concludes with someone's saying, "All this and more . . . tomorrow on the 700 Club."

Jimmy Swaggart is a somewhat older-style evangelist. Though he plays the piano quite well, sings sweetly, and uses the full range of television's resources, when he gets going he favors a kind of fire-and-brimstone approach. But because this is television, he often moderates his message with a dollop of ecumenism. For example, his sermon on the question, Are the

Jews practicing blasphemy? begins by assuring his audience that they are not, by recalling Jesus' bar mitzvah, and by insisting that Christians owe the Jews a considerable debt. It ends with his indicating that with the loss of their Temple in Biblical times, the Jews have somehow lost their way. His message suggests that they are rather to be pitied than despised but that, in any case, many of them are pretty nice people.

It is the perfect television sermon—theatrical, emotional, and in a curious way comforting, even to a Jewish viewer. For television—bless its heart—is not congenial to messages of naked hate. For one thing, you never know who is watching, so it is best not to be wildly offensive. For another, haters with reddened faces and demonic gestures merely look foolish on television, as Marshall McLuhan observed years ago and Senator Joseph McCarthy learned to his dismay. Television favors moods of conciliation and is at its best when substance of any kind is muted. (One must make an exception here for those instances when preachers, like Swaggart, turn to the subject of the Devil and secular humanism. Then they are quite uncompromising in the ferocity of their assaults, partly, one may assume, because neither the Devil nor secular humanists are included in the Nielsen Ratings. Neither are they inclined to watch.)

There are at present thirty-five television stations owned and operated by religious organizations, but every television station features religious programming of one sort or another. To prepare myself for writing this chapter, I watched forty-two hours of television's version of religion, mostly the shows of Robert Schuller, Oral Roberts, Jimmy Swaggart, Jerry Falwell, Jim Bakker and Pat Robertson. Forty-two hours were entirely unnecessary. Five would have provided me with all the conclusions, of which there are two, that are fairly to be drawn.

The first is that on television, religion, like everything else, is presented, quite simply and without apology, as an entertainment. Everything that makes religion an historic, profound and sacred human activity is stripped away; there is no ritual, no dogma, no tradition, no theology, and above all, no sense of spiritual transcendence. On these shows, the preacher is tops. God comes out as second banana.

The second conclusion is that this fact has more to do with the bias of television than with the deficiencies of these electronic preachers, as they are called. It is true enough that some of these men are uneducated, provincial and even bigoted. They certainly do not compare favorably with well-known evangelicals of an earlier period, such as Jonathan Edwards, George Whitefield and Charles Finney, who were men of great learning, theological subtlety and powerful expositional skills. Nonetheless, today's television preachers are probably not greatly different in their limitations from most earlier evangelicals or from many ministers today whose activities are confined to churches and synagogues. What makes these television preachers the enemy of religious experience is not so much *their* weaknesses but the weaknesses of the medium in which they work.

Most Americans, including preachers, have difficulty accepting the truth, if they think about it at all, that not all forms of discourse can be converted from one medium to another. It is naive to suppose that something that has been expressed in one form can be expressed in another without significantly changing its meaning, texture or value. Much prose translates fairly well from one language to another, but we know that poetry does not; we may get a rough idea of the sense of a translated poem but usually everything else is lost, especially that which makes it an object of beauty. The translation makes it into something it was not. To take another example: We may find it convenient to send a condolence card to a bereaved friend, but we delude ourselves if we believe that our card conveys the same meaning as our broken and whispered words when we are present. The card not only changes the words but eliminates the context from which the words take their meaning. Similarly, we delude ourselves if we believe that most everything a teacher normally does can be replicated with greater efficiency by a micro-computer. Perhaps some things can, but there is always the question, What is lost in the translation? The answer may even be: Everything that is significant about education.

Though it may be un-American to say it, not everything is *televisible*. Or to put it more precisely, what is televised is transformed from what it was to something else, which may or may not preserve its former essence. For the most part, television preachers have not seriously addressed this matter. They have assumed that what had formerly been done in a church or a tent, and face-to-face, can be done on television without loss of meaning, without changing the quality of the religious experience. Perhaps their failure to address the translation issue has its origin in the hubris engendered by the dazzling number of people to whom television gives them access.

"Television," Billy Graham has written, "is the most powerful tool of communication ever devised by man. Each of my prime-time 'specials' is now carried by nearly 300 stations across the U.S. and Canada, so that in a single telecast I preach to millions more than Christ did in his lifetime." [1] To this, Pat Robertson adds: "To say that the church shouldn't be involved with television is utter folly. The needs are the same, the message is the same, but the delivery can change. . . . It would be folly for the church not to get involved with the most formative force in America." [2]

This is gross technological naiveté. If the delivery is not the same, then the message, quite likely, is not the same. And if the context in which the message is experienced is altogether different from what it was in Jesus' time, we may assume that its social and psychological meaning is different, as well.

To come to the point, there are several characteristics of television and its surround that converge to make authentic religious experience impossible. The first has to do with the fact that there is no way to consecrate the space in which a television show is experienced. It is an essential condition of any traditional religious service that the space in which it is conducted must be invested with some measure of sacrality. Of course, a church or synagogue is designed as a place of ritual enactment so that almost anything that occurs there, even a bingo game, has a religious aura. But a religious service need not occur only in a church or synagogue. Almost any place will do, provided it is first decontaminated; that is, divested of its profane uses. This can be done by placing a cross on a wall, or candles on a table, or a sacred document in public view. Through such acts, a gymnasium or dining hall or hotel room can be transformed into a place of worship; a slice of space-time can be removed from the world of profane events, and be recreated into a reality that does not belong to our world. But for this transformation to be made, it is essential that certain rules of conduct be observed. There will be no eating or idle conversation, for example. One may be required to put on a skull cap or to kneel down at appropriate moments. Or simply to contemplate in silence. Our conduct must be congruent with the otherworldliness of the space. But this condition is not usually met when we are watching a religious television program. The activities in one's living room or bedroom or—God help us—one's kitchen are usually the same whether a religious program is being presented or "The A-Team" or "Dallas" is being presented. People will eat, talk, go to the bathroom, do push-ups or any of the things they are accustomed to doing in the presence of an animated television screen. If an audience is not immersed in an aura of mystery and symbolic otherworldliness, then it is unlikely that it can call forth the state of mind required for a nontrivial religious experience.

Moreover, the television screen itself has a strong bias toward a psychology of secularism. The screen is so saturated with our memories of profane events, so deeply associated with the commercial and entertainment worlds that it is difficult for it to be recreated as a frame for sacred events. Among other things, the viewer is at all times aware that a flick of the switch will produce a different and secular event on the screen—a hockey game, a commercial, a cartoon. Not only that, but both prior to and immediately following most religious programs, there are commercials, promos for popular shows, and a variety of other secular images and discourses, so that the main message of the screen itself is a continual promise of entertainment. Both the history and the ever-present possibilities of the television screen work against the idea that introspection or spiritual transcendence is desirable in its presence. The television screen wants you to remember that its imagery is always available for your amusement and pleasure.

The television preachers themselves are well aware of this. They know that their programs do not represent a discontinuity in commercial broadcasting but are merely part of an unbroken continuum. Indeed, many of these programs are presented at times other than traditional Sunday hours. Some of the more popular preachers are quite willing to go "head to head" with secular programs because they believe they can put on a more appealing show. Incidentally, the money to do this is no problem. Contributions to these shows run into the millions. It has been estimated that the total revenue of the electric church exceeds $500 million a year.

I mention this only to indicate why it is possible for these preachers to match the high production costs of any strictly commercial program. And match them they do. Most of the religious shows feature sparkling fountains, floral displays, choral groups and elaborate sets. All of them take as their model for staging some well-known commercial program. Jim Bakker, for example, uses "The Merv Griffin Show" as his guide. More than occasionally, programs are done "on location," in exotic locales with attractive and unfamiliar vistas.

In addition, exceedingly handsome people are usually in view, both on the stage and in the audience. Robert Schuller is particularly partial to celebrities, especially movie actors like Efrem Zimbalist, Jr., and Cliff Robertson, who have declared their allegiance to him. Not only does Schuller have celebrities on his show but his advertisements use their presence to attract an audience. Indeed, I think it fair to say that attracting an audience is the main goal of these programs, just as it is for "The A-Team" and "Dallas."

To achieve this goal, the most modern methods of marketing and promotion are abundantly used, such as offering free pamphlets, Bibles and gifts, and, in Jerry Falwell's case, two free "Jesus First" pins. The preachers are forthright about how they control the content of their preaching to maximize their ratings. You shall wait a very long time indeed if you wish to hear an electronic preacher refer to the difficulties a rich man will have in gaining access to heaven. The executive director of the National Religious Broadcasters Association sums up what he calls the unwritten law of all television preachers: "You can get your share of the audience only by offering people something they want." [3]

You will note, I am sure, that this is an unusual religious credo. There is no great religious leader—from the Buddha to Moses to Jesus to Mohammed to Luther—who offered people what they want. Only what they need. But television is not well suited to offering people what they need. It is "user friendly." It is too easy to turn off. It is at its most alluring when it speaks the language of dynamic visual imagery. It does not accommodate complex language or stringent demands. As a consequence, what is preached on television is not anything like the Sermon on the Mount. Religious programs are filled with good cheer. They celebrate affluence. Their featured players become celebrities. Though their messages are trivial, the shows have high ratings, or rather, *because* their messages are trivial, the shows have high ratings.

I believe I am not mistaken in saying that Christianity is a demanding and serious religion. When it is delivered as easy and amusing, it is another kind of religion altogether.

There are, of course, counterarguments to the claim that television degrades religion. Among them is that spectacle is hardly a stranger to religion. If one puts aside the Quakers and a few other austere sects, every religion tries to make itself appealing through art, music, icons and awe-inspiring ritual. The aesthetic dimension to religion is the source of its attraction to many people. This is especially true of Roman Catholicism and Judaism, which supply their congregants with haunting chants; magnificent robes and shawls; magical hats, wafers and wine; stained-glass windows; and the mysterious cadences of ancient languages. The difference between these accoutrements of religion and the floral displays, fountains and elaborate sets we see on television is that the former are not, in fact, accoutrements but integral parts of the history and doctrines of the religion itself; they require congregants to respond to them with suitable reverence. A Jew does not cover his head at prayer because a skull cap looks good on television. A Catholic does not light a votive candle to improve the look of the altar. Rabbis, priests and Presbyterian ministers do not, in the midst of a service, take testimony from movie stars to find out why they are religious people. The spectacle we find in true religions has as its purpose enchantment, not entertainment. The distinction is critical. By endowing things with magic, enchantment is the means through which we may gain access to sacredness. Entertainment is the means through which we distance ourselves from it.

The reply to this is that most of the religion available to us on television is "fundamentalist," which explicitly disdains ritual and theology in favor of direct communication with the Bible itself, that is, with God. Without ensnaring myself in a theological argument for which I am unprepared, I think it both fair and obvious to say that on television, God is a vague and subordinate character. Though His name is invoked repeatedly, the concreteness and persistence of the image of the preacher carries the clear message that it is he, not He, who must be worshipped. I do not mean to imply that the preacher wishes it to be so; only that the power of a close-up televised face, in color, makes idolatry a continual hazard. Television is, after all, a form of graven imagery far more alluring than a golden calf. I suspect (though I have no external evidence of it) that Catholic objections to Bishop Fulton Sheen's theatrical performances on television (of several years back) sprang from the impression that viewers were misdirecting their devotions, away from God and toward Bishop Sheen, whose piercing eyes, awesome cape and stately tones were as close a resemblance to a deity as charisma allows.

Television's strongest point is that it brings personalities into our hearts, not abstractions into our heads. That is why CBS' programs about the universe were called "Walter Cronkite's Universe." One would think that the grandeur of the universe needs no assistance from Walter Cronkite. One would think wrong. CBS knows that Walter Cronkite plays better on television than the Milky Way. And Jimmy Swaggart plays better than God. For God exists only in our minds, whereas Swaggart is *there*, to be seen, admired, adored. Which is why he is the star of the show. And why Billy Graham is a celebrity, and why Oral Roberts has his own university, and why Robert Schuller has a crystal cathedral all to himself. If I am not mistaken, the word for this is blasphemy.

There is a final argument that whatever criticisms may be made of televised religion, there remains the inescapable fact that it attracts viewers by the millions. This would appear to be the meaning of the statements, quoted earlier by Billy Graham and Pat Robertson, that there is a need for it among the multitude. To which the best reply I know was made by Hannah Arendt, who, in reflecting on the products of mass culture, wrote:

> This state of affairs, which indeed is equalled nowhere else in the world, can properly be called mass culture; its promoters are neither the masses nor their entertainers, but are those who try to

entertain the masses with what once was an authentic object of culture, or to persuade them that *Hamlet* can be as entertaining as *My Fair Lady*, and educational as well. The danger of mass education is precisely that it may become very entertaining indeed; there are many great authors of the past who have survived centuries of oblivion and neglect, but it is still an open question whether they will be able to survive an entertaining version of what they have to say.[4]

If we substitute the word "religion" for *Hamlet*, and the phrase "great religious traditions" for "great authors of the past," this quotation may stand as the decisive critique of televised religion. There is no doubt, in other words, that religion can be made entertaining. The question is, By doing so, do we destroy it as an "authentic object of culture"? And does the popularity of a religion that employs the full resources of vaudeville drive more traditional religious conceptions into manic and trivial displays? I have already referred to Cardinal O'Connor's embarrassing attempts to be well liked and amusing, and to a parish priest who cheerfully tries to add rock music to Catholic education. I know of one rabbi who has seriously proposed to his congregation that Luciano Pavarotti be engaged to sing Kol Nidre at a Yom Kippur service. He believes that the event would fill the synagogue as never before. Who can doubt it? But as Hannah Arendt would say, *that* is the problem, not a solution to one. As a member of the Commission on Theology, Education and the Electronic Media of the National Council of the Churches of Christ, I am aware of the deep concern among "established" Protestant religions about the tendency toward refashioning Protestant services so that they are more televisible. It is well understood at the National Council that the danger is not that religion has become the content of television shows but that television shows may become the content of religion.

9.

Reach Out and Elect Someone

In *The Last Hurrah*, Edwin O'Connor's fine novel about lusty party politics in Boston, Mayor Frank Skeffington tries to instruct his young nephew in the realities of political machinery. Politics, he tells him, is the greatest spectator sport in America. In 1966, Ronald Reagan used a different metaphor. "Politics," he said, "is just like show business." [1]

Although sports has now become a major branch of show business, it still contains elements that make Skeffington's vision of politics somewhat more encouraging than Reagan's. In any sport the standard of excellence is well known to both the players and spectators, and an athlete's reputation rises and falls by his or her proximity to that standard. Where an athlete stands in relation to it cannot be easily disguised or faked, which means that David Garth can do very little to improve the image of an outfielder with a .218 batting average. It also means that a public opinion poll on the question, Who is the best woman tennis player in the world?, is meaningless. The public's opinion has nothing to do with it. Martina Navratilova's serve provides the decisive answer.

One may also note that spectators at a sporting event are usually well aware of the rules of the game and the meaning of each piece of the action. There is no way for a batter who strikes out with the bases loaded to argue the spectators into believing that he has done a useful thing for his team (except, perhaps, by reminding them that he *could* have hit into a double play). The difference between hits and strike-outs, touchdowns and fumbles, aces and double faults cannot be blurred, even by the pomposities and malapropisms of a Howard Cosell. If politics were like a sporting event, there would be several virtues to attach to its name: clarity, honesty, excellence.

But what virtues attach to politics if Ronald Reagan is right? Show business is not entirely without an idea of excellence, but its main business is to please the crowd, and its principal instrument is artifice. If politics is like show business, then the idea is not to pursue excellence, clarity or honesty but to *appear* as if you are, which is another matter altogether. And what the other matter is can be expressed in one word: advertising. In Joe McGinnis' book about Richard Nixon's campaign in 1968, *The Selling of the President*, he said much of what needs to be said about politics and advertising, both in his title and in the book. But not quite all. For though the selling of a President is an astonishing and degrading thing, it is only part of a larger point: In America, the fundamental metaphor for political discourse is the television commercial.

The television commercial is the most peculiar and pervasive form of communication to issue forth from the electric plug. An American who has reached the age of forty will have seen well over one million television commercials in his or her lifetime, and has close to another million to go before the first Social Security check arrives. We may safely assume, therefore, that the television commercial has profoundly influenced American habits of thought. Certainly, there is no difficulty in demonstrating that it has become an important paradigm for the structure of every type of public discourse. My major purpose here is to show how it has devastated political discourse. But there may be some value in my pointing, first, to its effect on commerce itself.

By bringing together in compact form all of the arts of show business—music, drama, imagery, humor, celebrity—the television commercial has mounted the most serious assault on capitalist ideology since the publication of *Das Kapital*. To understand why, we must remind ourselves that capitalism, like science and liberal democracy, was an outgrowth of the Enlightenment. Its principal theorists, even its most prosperous practitioners, believed capitalism to be based on the idea that both buyer and seller are sufficiently mature, well informed and reasonable to engage in transactions of mutual self-interest. If greed was taken to be the fuel of the capitalist engine, then surely rationality was the driver. The theory states, in part, that competition in the marketplace requires that the buyer not only knows what is good for him but also what is good. If the seller produces nothing of value, as determined by a rational marketplace, then he loses out. It is the assumption of rationality among buyers that spurs competitors to become winners, and winners to keep on winning. Where it is assumed that a buyer is unable to make rational decisions, laws are passed to invalidate transactions, as, for example, those which prohibit children from making contracts. In America, there even exists in law a requirement that sellers must tell the truth about their products, for if the buyer has no protection from false claims, rational decision-making is seriously impaired.

Of course, the practice of capitalism has its contradictions. Cartels and monopolies, for example, undermine the theory. But television commercials make hash of it. To take the simplest example: To be rationally considered, any claim—commercial or otherwise—must be made in language. More precisely, it must take the form of a proposition, for that is the universe of discourse from which such words as "true" and "false" come. If that universe of discourse is discarded, then the application of empirical tests, logical analysis or any of the other instruments of reason are impotent.

The move away from the use of propositions in commercial advertising began at the end of the nineteenth century. But it was not until the 1950's that the television commercial made linguistic discourse obsolete as the basis for product decisions. By substituting images for claims, the pictorial commercial made emotional appeal, not tests of truth, the basis of consumer decisions. The distance between rationality and advertising is now so wide that it is difficult to remember that there once existed a connection between them. Today, on television commercials, propositions are as scarce as unattractive people. The truth or falsity of an advertiser's claim is simply not an issue. A McDonald's commercial, for example, is not a series of testable, logically ordered assertions. It is a drama—a mythology, if you will—of handsome people selling, buying and eating hamburgers, and being driven to near ecstasy by their good fortune. No claims are made, except those the viewer projects onto or infers from the drama. One can like or dislike a television commercial, of course. But one cannot refute it.

Indeed, we may go this far: The television commercial is not at all about the character of products to be consumed. It is about the character of the consumers of products. Images of movie stars and famous athletes, of serene lakes and macho fishing trips, of elegant dinners and romantic interludes, of happy families packing their station wagons for a picnic in the country— these tell nothing about the products being sold. But they tell everything about the fears, fancies and dreams of those who might buy them. What the advertiser needs to know is not what is right about the product but what is wrong about the buyer. And so, the balance of business expenditures shifts from *product* research to *market* research. The television commercial has oriented business away from making products of value and toward making consumers feel valuable, which means that the business of business has now become pseudo-therapy. The consumer is a patient assured by psycho-dramas.

All of this would come as a great surprise to Adam Smith, just as the transformation of politics would be equally surprising to the redoubtable George Orwell. It is true, as George Steiner has remarked, that Orwell thought of Newspeak as originating, in part, from "the verbiage of commercial advertising." But when Orwell wrote in his famous essay "The Politics of the English

Language'' that politics has become a matter of ''defending the indefensible,'' he was assuming that politics would remain a distinct, although corrupted, mode of discourse. His contempt was aimed at those politicians who would use sophisticated versions of the age-old arts of double-think, propaganda and deceit. That the defense of the indefensible would be conducted as a form of amusement did not occur to him. He feared the politician as deceiver, not as entertainer.

The television commercial has been the chief instrument in creating the modern methods of presenting political ideas. It has accomplished this in two ways. The first is by requiring its form to be used in political campaigns. It is not necessary, I take it, to say very much about this method. Everyone has noticed and worried in varying degrees about it, including former New York City mayor John Lindsay, who has proposed that political ''commercials'' be prohibited. Even television commentators have brought it to our attention, as for example, Bill Moyers in ''The Thirty-second President,'' a documentary on his excellent television series ''A Walk Through the 20th Century.'' My own awakening to the power of the television commercial as political discourse came as a result of a personal experience of a few years back, when I played a minuscule role in Ramsey Clark's Senate campaign against Jacob Javits in New York. A great believer in the traditional modes of political discourse, Clark prepared a small library of carefully articulated position papers on a variety of subjects from race relations to nuclear power to the Middle East. He filled each paper with historical background, economic and political facts, and, I thought, an enlightened sociological perspective. He might as well have drawn cartoons. In fact, Jacob Javits did draw cartoons, in a manner of speaking. If Javits had a carefully phrased position on any issue, the fact was largely unknown. He built his campaign on a series of thirty-second television commercials in which he used visual imagery, in much the same way as a McDonald's commercial, to project himself as a man of experience, virtue and piety. For all I know, Javits believed as strongly in reason as did Ramsey Clark. But he believed more strongly in retaining his seat in the Senate. And he knew full well in what century we are living. He understood that in a world of television and other visual media, "political knowledge" means having pictures in your head more than having words. The record will show that this insight did not fail him. He won the election by the largest plurality in New York State history. And I will not labor the commonplace that any serious candidate for high political office in America requires the services of an image manager to design the kinds of pictures that will lodge in the public's collective head. I will want to return to the implications of "image politics" but it is necessary, before that, to discuss the second method by which the television commercial shapes political discourse.

Because the television commercial is the single most voluminous form of public communication in our society, it was inevitable that Americans would accommodate themselves to the philosophy of television commercials. By "accommodate," I mean that we accept them as a normal and plausible form of discourse. By "philosophy," I mean that the television commercial has embedded in it certain assumptions about the nature of communication that run counter to those of other media, especially the printed word. For one thing, the commercial insists on an unprecedented brevity of expression. One may even say, instancy. A sixty-second commercial is prolix; thirty seconds is longer than most; fifteen to twenty seconds is about average. This is a brash and startling structure for communication since, as I remarked earlier, the commercial always addresses itself to the psychological needs of the viewer. Thus it is not merely therapy. It is instant therapy. Indeed, it puts forward a psychological theory of unique axioms: The commercial asks us to believe that all problems are solvable, that they are solvable fast, and that they are solvable fast through the interventions of technology, techniques and chemistry. This is, of course, a preposterous theory about the roots of discontent, and would ap-

pear so to anyone hearing or reading it. But the commercial
disdains exposition, for that takes time and invites argument. It
is a very bad commercial indeed that engages the viewer in
wondering about the validity of the point being made. That is
why most commercials use the literary device of the pseudo-
parable as a means of doing their work. Such "parables" as The
Ring Around the Collar, The Lost Traveler's Checks and The
Phone Call from the Son Far Away not only have irrefutable
emotional power but, like Biblical parables, are unambiguously
didactic. The television commercial is about products only in
the sense that the story of Jonah is about the anatomy of
whales, which is to say, it isn't. Which is to say further, it is
about how one ought to live one's life. Moreover, commercials
have the advantage of vivid visual symbols through which we
may easily learn the lessons being taught. Among those lessons
are that short and simple messages are preferable to long and
complex ones; that drama is to be preferred over exposition;
that being sold solutions is better than being confronted with
questions about problems. Such beliefs would naturally have
implications for our orientation to political discourse; that is to
say, we may begin to accept as normal certain assumptions
about the political domain that either derive from or are amplified by the television commercial. For example, a person who
has seen one million television commercials might well believe
that all political problems have fast solutions through simple
measures—or ought to. Or that complex language is not to be
trusted, and that all problems lend themselves to theatrical expression. Or that argument is in bad taste, and leads only to an
intolerable uncertainty. Such a person may also come to believe
that it is not necessary to draw any line between politics and
other forms of social life. Just as a television commercial will
use an athlete, an actor, a musician, a novelist, a scientist or a
countess to speak for the virtues of a product in no way within
their domain of expertise, television also frees politicians from
the limited field of their own expertise. Political figures may

show up anywhere, at any time, doing anything, without being thought odd, presumptuous, or in any way out of place. Which is to say, they have become assimilated into the general television culture as celebrities.

Being a celebrity is quite different from being well known. Harry Truman was well known but he was not a celebrity. Whenever the public saw him or heard him, Truman was talking politics. It takes a very rich imagination to envision Harry Truman or, for that matter, his wife, making a guest appearance on "The Goldbergs" or "I Remember Mama." Politics and politicians had nothing to do with these shows, which people watched for amusement, not to familiarize themselves with political candidates and issues.

It is difficult to say exactly when politicians began to put themselves forward, intentionally, as sources of amusement. In the 1950's, Senator Everett Dirksen appeared as a guest on "What's My Line?" When he was running for office, John F. Kennedy allowed the television cameras of Ed Murrow's "Person to Person" to invade his home. When he was not running for office, Richard Nixon appeared for a few seconds on "Laugh-In," an hour-long comedy show based on the format of a television commercial. By the 1970's, the public had started to become accustomed to the notion that political figures were to be taken as part of the world of show business. In the 1980's came the deluge. Vice-presidential candidate William Miller did a commercial for American Express. So did the star of the Watergate Hearings, Senator Sam Ervin. Former President Gerald Ford joined with former Secretary of State Henry Kissinger for brief roles on "Dynasty." Massachusetts Governor Mike Dukakis appeared on "St. Elsewhere." Speaker of the House Tip O'Neill did a stint on "Cheers." Consumer advocate Ralph Nader, George McGovern and Mayor Edward Koch hosted "Saturday Night Live." Koch also played the role of a fight manager in a made-for-television movie starring James Cagney. Mrs. Nancy Reagan appeared on "Diff'rent Strokes." Would anyone be surprised if Gary Hart turned up on "Hill Street Blues"? Or if Geraldine Ferraro played a small role as a Queens housewife in a Francis Coppola film?

Although it may go too far to say that the politician-as-celebrity has, by itself, made political parties irrelevant, there is certainly a conspicuous correlation between the rise of the former and the decline of the latter. Some readers may remember when voters barely knew who the candidate was and, in any case, were not preoccupied with his character and personal life. As a young man, I balked one November at voting for a Democratic mayoralty candidate who, it seemed to me, was both unintelligent and corrupt. "What has that to do with it?" my father protested. "*All* Democratic candidates are unintelligent and corrupt. Do you want the Republicans to win?" He meant to say that intelligent voters favored the party that best represented their economic interests and sociological perspective. To vote for the "best man" seemed to him an astounding and naive irrelevance. He never doubted that there were good men among Republicans. He merely understood that they did not speak for his class. He shared, with an unfailing eye, the perspective of Big Tim Sullivan, a leader of New York's Tammany Hall in its glory days. As Terence Moran recounts in his essay, "Politics 1984," Sullivan was once displeased when brought the news that the vote in his precinct was 6,382 for the Democrat and two for the Republican. In evaluating this disappointing result, Sullivan remarked, "Sure, didn't Kelly come to me to say his wife's cousin was running on the Republican line and didn't I, in the interests of domestic tranquility, give him leave to vote Republican? But what I want to know is, who else voted Republican?"[2]

I will not argue here the wisdom of this point of view. There may be a case for choosing the best man over party (although I know of none). The point is that television does not reveal who the best man is. In fact, television makes impossible the determination of who is better than whom, if we mean by "better" such things as more capable in negotiation, more imaginative in executive skill, more knowledgeable about international affairs, more understanding of the interrelations of economic systems, and so on. The reason has, almost entirely, to do with "image." But not because politicians are preoccupied with presenting themselves in the best possible light. After all, who isn't? It is a rare and deeply disturbed person who does not wish to project a favorable image. But television gives image a bad name. For on television the politician does not so much offer the audience an image of himself, as offer himself as an image of the audience. And therein lies one of the most powerful influences of the television commercial on political discourse.

To understand how image politics works on television, we may use as an entry point the well-known commercial from which this chapter takes the first half of its title. I refer to the Bell Telephone romances, created by Mr. Steve Horn, in which we are urged to "Reach Out and Touch Someone." The "someone" is usually a relative who lives in Denver or Los Angeles or Atlanta—in any case, very far from where we are, and who, in a good year, we will be lucky to see on Thanksgiving Day. The "someone" used to play a daily and vital role in our lives; that is to say, used to be a member of the family. Though American culture stands vigorously opposed to the idea of family, there nonetheless still exists a residual nag that something essential to our lives is lost when we give it up. Enter Mr. Horn's commercials. These are thirty-second homilies concerned to provide a new definition of intimacy in which the telephone wire will take the place of old-fashioned co-presence. Even further, these commercials intimate a new conception of family cohesion for a nation of kinsmen who have been split asunder by automobiles, jet aircraft and other instruments of family suicide. In analyzing these commercials, Jay Rosen makes the following observation: "Horn isn't interested in saying anything, he has no message to get across. His goal is not to provide information about Bell, but to somehow bring out from the broken ties of millions of American lives a feeling which might focus on the telephone. . . . Horn does not express himself. You do not express yourself. Horn expresses you." [3]

This is the lesson of all great television commercials: They provide a slogan, a symbol or a focus that creates for viewers a comprehensive and compelling image of themselves. In the shift from party politics to television politics, the same goal is sought. We are not permitted to know who is best at being President or Governor or Senator, but whose image is best in touching and soothing the deep reaches of our discontent. We look at the television screen and ask, in the same voracious way as the Queen in *Snow White and the Seven Dwarfs,* "Mirror, mirror on the wall, who is the fairest one of all?" We are inclined to vote for those whose personality, family life, and style, as imaged on the screen, give back a better answer than the Queen received. As Xenophanes remarked twenty-five centuries ago, men always make their gods in their own image. But to this, television politics has added a new wrinkle: Those who would be gods refashion themselves into images the viewers would have them be.

And so, while image politics preserves the idea of self-interest voting, it alters the meaning of "self-interest." Big Tim Sullivan and my father voted for the party that represented their interests, but "interests" meant to them something tangible—patronage, preferential treatment, protection from bureaucracy, support for one's union or community, Thanksgiving turkeys for indigent families. Judged by this standard, blacks may be the only sane voters left in America. Most of the rest of us vote our interests, but they are largely symbolic ones, which is to say, of a psychological nature. Like television commercials, image politics is a form of therapy, which is why so much of it is charm, good looks, celebrity and personal disclosure. It is a sobering thought to recall that there are no photographs of Abraham Lincoln smiling, that his wife was in all likelihood a psychopath, and that he was subject to lengthy fits of depression. He would hardly have been well suited for image politics. We do not want our mirrors to be so dark and so far from amusing. What I am saying is that just as the television commercial empties itself of authentic product information so that it can do its psychological work, image politics empties itself of authentic political substance for the same reason.

It follows from this that history can play no significant role in image politics. For history is of value only to someone who takes seriously the notion that there are patterns in the past which may provide the present with nourishing traditions. "The past is a world," Thomas Carlyle said, "and not a void of grey haze." But he wrote this at a time when the book was the principal medium of serious public discourse. A book is *all* history. Everything about it takes one back in time—from the way it is produced to its linear mode of exposition to the fact that the past tense is its most comfortable form of address. As no other medium before or since, the book promotes a sense of a coherent and usable past. In a conversation of books, history, as Carlyle understood it, is not only a world but a living world. It is the present that is shadowy.

But television is a speed-of-light medium, a present-centered medium. Its grammar, so to say, permits no access to the past. Everything presented in moving pictures is experienced as happening "now," which is why we must be told *in language* that a videotape we are seeing was made months before. Moreover, like its forefather, the telegraph, television needs to move fragments of information, not to collect and organize them. Carlyle was more prophetic than he could imagine: The literal gray haze that is the background void on all television screens is an apt metaphor of the notion of history the medium puts forward. In the Age of Show Business and image politics, political discourse is emptied not only of ideological content but of historical content, as well.

Czeslaw Milosz, winner of the 1980 Nobel Prize for Literature, remarked in his acceptance speech in Stockholm that our age is characterized by a "refusal to remember"; he cited, among other things, the shattering fact that there are now more than one hundred books in print that deny that the Holocaust ever took place. The historian Carl Schorske has, in my opinion, circled closer to the truth by noting that the modern mind has grown indifferent to history because history has become useless to it; in other words, it is not obstinacy or ignorance but a sense of irrelevance that leads to the diminution of history. Television's Bill Moyers inches still closer when he says, "I worry that my own business . . . helps to make this an anxious age of agitated amnesiacs. . . . We Americans seem to know everything about the last twenty-four hours but very little of the last sixty centuries or the last sixty years."[4] Terence Moran, I believe, lands on the target in saying that with media whose structure is biased toward furnishing images and fragments, we are deprived of access to an historical perspective. In the absence of continuity and context, he says, "bits of information cannot be integrated into an intelligent and consistent whole."[5] We do not refuse to remember; neither do we find it exactly useless to remember. Rather, we are being rendered unfit to remember. For if remembering is to be something more than nostalgia, it requires a contextual basis—a theory, a vision, a metaphor—*something* within which facts can be organized and patterns discerned. The politics of image and instantaneous news provides no such context, is, in fact, hampered by attempts to provide any. A mirror records only what you are wearing today. It is silent about yesterday. With television, we vault ourselves into a continuous, incoherent present. "History," Henry Ford said, "is bunk." Henry Ford was a typographic optimist. "History," the Electric Plug replies, "doesn't exist."

If these conjectures make sense, then in this Orwell was wrong once again, at least for the Western democracies. He envisioned the demolition of history, but believed that it would be accomplished by the state; that some equivalent of the Ministry of Truth would systematically banish inconvenient facts and destroy the records of the past. Certainly, this is the way of the Soviet Union, our modern-day Oceania. But as Huxley more accurately foretold it, nothing so crude as all that is required. Seemingly benign technologies devoted to providing the populace with a politics of image, instancy and therapy may disappear history just as effectively, perhaps more permanently, and without objection.

We ought also to look to Huxley, not Orwell, to understand the threat that television and other forms of imagery pose to the foundation of liberal democracy—namely, to freedom of information. Orwell quite reasonably supposed that the state, through naked suppression, would control the flow of information, particularly by the banning of books. In this prophecy, Orwell had history strongly on his side. For books have always been subjected to censorship in varying degrees wherever they have been an important part of the communication landscape. In ancient China, the *Analects* of Confucius were ordered destroyed by Emperor Chi Huang Ti. Ovid's banishment from Rome by Augustus was in part a result of his having written *Ars Amatoria*. Even in Athens, which set enduring standards of intellectual excellence, books were viewed with alarm. In *Areopagitica*, Milton provides an excellent review of the many examples of book censorship in Classical Greece, including the case of Protagoras, whose books were burned because he began one of his discourses with the confession that he did not know whether or not there were gods. But Milton is careful to observe that in all the cases before his own time, there were only two types of books that, as he puts it, ''the magistrate cared to take notice of'': books that were blasphemous and books that were libelous. Milton stresses this point because, writing almost two hundred years after Gutenberg, he knew that the magistrates of his own era, if unopposed, would disallow books of every conceivable subject matter. Milton knew, in other words, that it was in the printing press that censorship had found its true métier; that, in fact, information and ideas did not become a profound cultural problem until the maturing of the Age of Print. Whatever dangers there may be in a word that is written, such a word is a hundred times more dangerous when stamped by a press. And the problem posed by typography was recognized early; for example, by Henry VIII, whose Star Chamber was authorized to deal with wayward books. It continued to be recognized by Elizabeth I, the Stuarts, and many other post-Gutenberg monarchs, including Pope Paul IV, in whose reign the first *Index Librorum Prohibitorum* was drawn. To paraphrase David Riesman only slightly, in a world of printing, information is the gunpowder of the mind; hence come the censors in their austere robes to dampen the explosion.

Thus, Orwell envisioned that (1) government control over (2) printed matter posed a serious threat for Western democracies. He was wrong on both counts. (He was, of course, right on both counts insofar as Russia, China and other pre-electronic cultures are concerned.) Orwell was, in effect, addressing himself to a problem of the Age of Print—in fact, to the same problem addressed by the men who wrote the United States Constitution. The Constitution was composed at a time when most free men had access to their communities through a leaflet, a newspaper or the spoken word. They were quite well positioned to share their political ideas with each other in forms and contexts over which they had competent control. Therefore, their greatest worry was the possibility of government tyranny. The Bill of Rights is largely a prescription for preventing government from restricting the flow of information and ideas. But the Founding Fathers did not foresee that tyranny by government might be superseded by another sort of problem altogether, namely, the corporate state, which through television now controls the flow of public discourse in America. I raise no strong objection to this fact (at least not here) and have no intention of launching into a standard-brand complaint against the corporate state. I merely note the fact with apprehension, as did George Gerbner, Dean of the Annenberg School of Communication, when he wrote:

Television is the new state religion run by a private Ministry of Culture (the three networks), offering a universal curriculum for all people, financed by a form of hidden taxation without representation. You pay when you wash, not when you watch, and whether or not you care to watch. . . .[6]

Earlier in the same essay, Gerbner said:

Liberation cannot be accomplished by turning [television] off. Television is for most people the most attractive thing going any time of the day or night. We live in a world in which the vast majority will not turn off. If we don't get the message from the tube, we get it through other people.

I do not think Professor Gerbner meant to imply in these sentences that there is a conspiracy to take charge of our symbolic world by the men who run the "Ministry of Culture." I even suspect he would agree with me that if the faculty of the Annenberg School of Communication were to take over the three networks, viewers would hardly notice the difference. I believe he means to say—and in any case, *I* do—that in the Age of Television, our information environment is completely different from what it was in 1783; that we have less to fear from government restraints than from television glut; that, in fact, we have no way of protecting ourselves from information disseminated by corporate America; and that, therefore, the battles for liberty must be fought on different terrains from where they once were.

For example, I would venture the opinion that the traditional civil libertarian opposition to the banning of books from school libraries and from school curricula is now largely irrelevant. Such acts of censorship are annoying, of course, and must be opposed. But they are trivial. Even worse, they are distracting, in that they divert civil libertarians from confronting those questions that have to do with the claims of new technologies.

To put it plainly, a student's freedom to read is not seriously injured by someone's banning a book on Long Island or in Anaheim or anyplace else. But as Gerbner suggests, television clearly does impair the student's freedom to read, and it does so with innocent hands, so to speak. Television does not ban books, it simply displaces them.

The fight against censorship is a nineteenth-century issue which was largely won in the twentieth. What we are confronted with now is the problem posed by the economic and symbolic structure of television. Those who run television do not limit our access to information but in fact widen it. Our Ministry of Culture is Huxleyan, not Orwellian. It does everything possible to encourage us to watch continuously. But what we watch is a medium which presents information in a form that renders it simplistic, nonsubstantive, nonhistorical and noncontextual; that is to say, information packaged as entertainment. In America, we are never denied the opportunity to amuse ourselves.

Tyrants of all varieties have always known about the value of providing the masses with amusements as a means of pacifying discontent. But most of them could not have even hoped for a situation in which the masses would ignore that which does not amuse. That is why tyrants have always relied, and still do, on censorship. Censorship, after all, is the tribute tyrants pay to the assumption that a public knows the difference between serious discourse and entertainment—and cares. How delighted would be all the kings, czars and führers of the past (and commissars of the present) to know that censorship is not a necessity when all political discourse takes the form of a jest.

IO.

Teaching as an Amusing Activity

There could not have been a safer bet when it began in 1969 than that "Sesame Street" would be embraced by children, parents and educators. Children loved it because they were raised on television commercials, which they intuitively knew were the most carefully crafted entertainments on television. To those who had not yet been to school, even to those who had just started, the idea of being *taught* by a series of commercials did not seem peculiar. And that television should entertain them was taken as a matter of course.

Parents embraced "Sesame Street" for several reasons, among them that it assuaged their guilt over the fact that they could not or would not restrict their children's access to television. "Sesame Street" appeared to justify allowing a four- or five-year-old to sit transfixed in front of a television screen for unnatural periods of time. Parents were eager to hope that television could teach their children something other than which breakfast cereal has the most crackle. At the same time, "Sesame Street" relieved them of the responsibility of teaching their pre-school children how to read—no small matter in a culture where children are apt to be considered a nuisance. They could also plainly see that in spite of its faults, "Sesame Street" was entirely consonant with the prevailing spirit of America. Its use of cute puppets, celebrities, catchy tunes, and rapid-fire editing was certain to give pleasure to the children and would therefore serve as adequate preparation for their entry into a fun-loving culture.

As for educators, they generally approved of "Sesame Street," too. Contrary to common opinion, they are apt to find new methods congenial, especially if they are told that education can be accomplished more efficiently by means of the new techniques. (That is why such ideas as "teacher-proof" textbooks, standardized tests, and, now, micro-computers have been welcomed into the classroom.) "Sesame Street" appeared to be an imaginative aid in solving the growing problem of teaching Americans how to read, while, at the same time, encouraging children to love school.

We now know that "Sesame Street" encourages children to love school only if school is like "Sesame Street." Which is to say, we now know that "Sesame Street" undermines what the traditional idea of schooling represents. Whereas a classroom is a place of social interaction, the space in front of a television set is a private preserve. Whereas in a classroom, one may ask a teacher questions, one can ask nothing of a television screen. Whereas school is centered on the development of language, television demands attention to images. Whereas attending school is a legal requirement, watching television is an act of choice. Whereas in school, one fails to attend to the teacher at the risk of punishment, no penalties exist for failing to attend to the television screen. Whereas to behave oneself in school means to observe rules of public decorum, television watching requires no such observances, has no concept of public decorum. Whereas in a classroom, fun is never more than a means to an end, on television it is the end in itself.

Yet "Sesame Street" and its progeny, "The Electric Company," are not to be blamed for laughing the traditional classroom out of existence. If the classroom now begins to seem a stale and flat environment for learning, the inventors of television itself are to blame, not the Children's Television Workshop. We can hardly expect those who want to make good television shows to concern themselves with what the classroom is for. They are concerned with what television is for. This does not mean that "Sesame Street" is not educational. It is, in fact, nothing but educational—in the sense that every television show is educational. Just as reading a book—any kind of book —promotes a particular orientation toward learning, watching a television show does the same. "The Little House on the Prairie," "Cheers" and "The Tonight Show" are as effective as "Sesame Street" in promoting what might be called the television style of learning. And this style of learning is, by its nature, hostile to what has been called book-learning or its hand-maiden, school-learning. If we are to blame "Sesame Street" for anything, it is for the pretense that it is any ally of the class-room. That, after all, has been its chief claim on foundation and public money. As a television show, and a good one, "Sesame Street" does not encourage children to love school or anything about school. It encourages them to love television.

Moreover, it is important to add that whether or not "Sesame Street" teaches children their letters and numbers is entirely ir-relevant. We may take as our guide here John Dewey's observa-tion that the content of a lesson is the least important thing about learning. As he wrote in *Experience and Education:* "Per-haps the greatest of all pedagogical fallacies is the notion that a person learns only what he is studying at the time. Collateral learning in the way of formation of enduring attitudes . . . may be and often is more important than the spelling lesson or lesson in geography or history. . . . For these attitudes are fun-damentally what count in the future."[1] In other words, the most important thing one learns is always something about *how* one learns. As Dewey wrote in another place, we learn what we do. Television educates by teaching children to do what television-viewing requires of them. And that is as precisely re-mote from what a classroom requires of them as reading a book is from watching a stage show.

Although one would not know it from consulting various re-cent proposals on how to mend the educational system, this point—that reading books and watching television differ entirely in what they imply about learning—is the primary educational issue in America today. America is, in fact, the leading case in point of what may be thought of as the third great crisis in Western education. The first occurred in the fifth century B.C., when Athens underwent a change from an oral culture to an alphabet-writing culture. To understand what this meant, we must read Plato. The second occurred in the sixteenth century, when Europe underwent a radical transformation as a result of the printing press. To understand what this meant, we must read John Locke. The third is happening now, in America, as a result of the electronic revolution, particularly the invention of television. To understand what this means, we must read Marshall McLuhan.

We face the rapid dissolution of the assumptions of an education organized around the slow-moving printed word, and the equally rapid emergence of a new education based on the speed-of-light electronic image. The classroom is, at the moment, still tied to the printed word, although that connection is rapidly weakening. Meanwhile, television forges ahead, making no concessions to its great technological predecessor, creating new conceptions of knowledge and how it is acquired. One is entirely justified in saying that the major educational enterprise now being undertaken in the United States is not happening in its classrooms but in the home, in front of the television set, and under the jurisdiction not of school administrators and teachers but of network executives and entertainers. I don't mean to imply that the situation is a result of a conspiracy or even that those who control television want this responsibility. I mean only to say that, like the alphabet or the printing press, television has by its power to control the time, attention and cognitive habits of our youth gained the power to control their education.

This is why I think it accurate to call television a curriculum. As I understand the word, a curriculum is a specially constructed information system whose purpose is to influence, teach, train or cultivate the mind and character of youth. Television, of course, does exactly that, and does it relentlessly. In so doing, it competes successfully with the school curriculum. By which I mean, it damn near obliterates it.

Having devoted an earlier book, *Teaching as a Conserving Activity,* to a detailed examination of the antagonistic nature of the two curriculums—television and school—I will not burden the reader or myself with a repetition of that analysis. But I would like to recall two points that I feel I did not express forcefully enough in that book and that happen to be central to this one. I refer, first, to the fact that television's principal contribution to educational philosophy is the idea that teaching and entertainment are inseparable. This entirely original conception is to be found nowhere in educational discourses, from Confucius to Plato to Cicero to Locke to John Dewey. In searching the literature of education, you will find it said by some that children will learn best when they are interested in what they are learning. You will find it said—Plato and Dewey emphasized this —that reason is best cultivated when it is rooted in robust emotional ground. You will even find some who say that learning is best facilitated by a loving and benign teacher. But no one has ever said or implied that significant learning is effectively, durably and truthfully achieved when education is entertainment. Education philosophers have assumed that becoming acculturated is difficult because it necessarily involves the imposition of restraints. They have argued that there must be a sequence to learning, that perseverance and a certain measure of perspiration are indispensable, that individual pleasures must frequently be submerged in the interests of group cohesion, and that learning to be critical and to think conceptually and rigorously do not come easily to the young but are hard-fought victories. Indeed, Cicero remarked that the purpose of education is to free the student from the tyranny of the present, which cannot be pleasurable for those, like the young, who are struggling hard to do the opposite—that is, accommodate themselves to the present.

Television offers a delicious and, as I have said, original alternative to all of this. We might say there are three commandments that form the philosophy of the education which television offers. The influence of these commandments is observable in every type of television programming—from "Sesame Street" to the documentaries of "Nova" and "The National Geographic" to "Fantasy Island" to MTV. The commandments are as follows:

Thou shalt have no prerequisites

Every television program must be a complete package in itself. No previous knowledge is to be required. There must not be even a hint that learning is hierarchical, that it is an edifice constructed on a foundation. The learner must be allowed to enter at any point without prejudice. This is why you shall never hear or see a television program begin with the caution that if the viewer has not seen the previous programs, this one will be meaningless. Television is a nongraded curriculum and excludes no viewer for any reason, at any time. In other words, in doing away with the idea of sequence and continuity in education, television undermines the idea that sequence and continuity have anything to do with thought itself.

Thou shalt induce no perplexity

In television teaching, perplexity is a superhighway to low ratings. A perplexed learner is a learner who will turn to another station. This means that there must be nothing that has to be remembered, studied, applied or, worst of all, endured. It is assumed that any information, story or idea can be made immediately accessible, since the contentment, not the growth, of the learner is paramount.

Thou shalt avoid exposition like the ten plagues visited upon Egypt

Of all the enemies of television-teaching, including continuity and perplexity, none is more formidable than exposition. Arguments, hypotheses, discussions, reasons, refutations or any of the traditional instruments of reasoned discourse turn television into radio or, worse, third-rate printed matter. Thus, television-teaching always takes the form of story-telling, conducted through dynamic images and supported by music. This is as characteristic of "Star Trek" as it is of "Cosmos," of "Diff'rent Strokes" as of "Sesame Street," of commercials as of "Nova." Nothing will be taught on television that cannot be both visualized and placed in a theatrical context.

The name we may properly give to an education without prerequisites, perplexity and exposition is entertainment. And when one considers that save for sleeping there is no activity that occupies more of an American youth's time than television-viewing, we cannot avoid the conclusion that a massive reorientation toward learning is now taking place. Which leads to the second point I wish to emphasize: The consequences of this reorientation are to be observed not only in the decline of the potency of the classroom but, paradoxically, in the refashioning of the classroom into a place where both teaching and learning are intended to be vastly amusing activities.

I have already referred to the experiment in Philadelphia in which the classroom is reconstituted as a rock concert. But this is only the silliest example of an attempt to define education as a mode of entertainment. Teachers, from primary grades through college, are increasing the visual stimulation of their lessons; are reducing the amount of exposition their students must cope with; are relying less on reading and writing assignments; and are reluctantly concluding that the principal means by which student interest may be engaged is entertainment. With no difficulty I could fill the remaining pages of this chapter with examples of teachers' efforts—in some instances, unconscious—to make their classrooms into second-rate television shows. But I will rest my case with "The Voyage of the Mimi," which may be taken as a synthesis, if not an apotheosis, of the New Education. "The Voyage of the Mimi" is the name of an expensive science and mathematics project that has brought together some of the most prestigious institutions in the field of education—the United States Department of Education, the Bank Street College of Education, the Public Broadcasting System, and the publishing firm Holt, Rinehart and Winston. The project was made possible by a $3.65 million grant from the Department of Education, which is always on the alert to put its money where the future is. And the future is "The Voyage of the Mimi." To describe the project succinctly, I quote from four paragraphs in *The New York Times* of August 7, 1984:

> Organized around a twenty-six-unit television series that depicts the adventures of a floating whale-research laboratory, [the project] combines television viewing with lavishly illustrated books and computer games that simulate the way scientists and navigators work. . . .
>
> "The Voyage of the Mimi" is built around fifteen-minute television programs that depict the adventures of four young people who accompany two scientists and a crusty sea captain on a voyage to monitor the behavior of humpback whales off the coast of Maine. The crew of the converted tuna trawler navigates the ship, tracks down the whales and struggles to survive on an uninhabited island after a storm damages the ship's hull. . . .
>
> Each dramatic episode is then followed by a fifteen-minute documentary on related themes. One such documentary involved a visit by one of the teen-age actors to Ted Taylor, a nuclear physicist in Greenport, L.I., who has devised a way of purifying sea water by freezing it.

The television programs, which teachers are free to record off the air and use at their convenience, are supplemented by a series of books and computer exercises that pick up four academic themes that emerge naturally from the story line: map and navigational skills, whales and their environment, ecological systems and computer literacy.

The television programs have been broadcast over PBS; the books and computer software have been provided by Holt, Rinehart and Winston; the educational expertise by the faculty of the Bank Street College. Thus, "The Voyage of the Mimi" is not to be taken lightly. As Frank Withrow of the Department of Education remarked, "We consider it the flagship of what we are doing. It is a model that others will begin to follow." Everyone involved in the project is enthusiastic, and extraordinary claims of its benefits come trippingly from their tongues. Janice Trebbi Richards of Holt, Rinehart and Winston asserts, "Research shows that learning increases when information is presented in a dramatic setting, and television can do this better than any other medium." Officials of the Department of Education claim that the appeal of integrating three media—television, print, and computers—lies in their potential for cultivating higher-order thinking skills. And Mr. Withrow is quoted as saying that projects like "The Voyage of the Mimi" could mean great financial savings, that in the long run "it is cheaper than anything else we do." Mr. Withrow also suggested that there are many ways of financing such projects. "With 'Sesame Street,'" he said, "it took five or six years, but eventually you can start bringing in the money with T-shirts and cookie jars."

We may start thinking about what "The Voyage of the Mimi" signifies by recalling that the idea is far from original. What is here referred to as "integrating three media" or a "multi-media presentation" was once called "audio-visual aids," used by teachers for years, usually for the modest purpose of enhancing student interest in the curriculum. Moreover, several years ago, the Office of Education (as the Department was then called) supplied funds to WNET for a similarly designed project called "Watch Your Mouth," a series of television dramatizations in which young people inclined to misuse the English language fumbled their way through a variety of social problems. Linguists and educators prepared lessons for teachers to use in conjunction with each program. The dramatizations were compelling—although not nearly as good as "Welcome Back, Kotter," which had the unassailable advantage of John Travolta's charisma—but there exists no evidence that students who were required to view "Watch Your Mouth" increased their competence in the use of the English language. Indeed, since there is no shortage of mangled English on everyday commercial television, one wondered at the time why the United States government would have paid anyone to go to the trouble of producing additional ineptitudes as a source of classroom study. A videotape of any of David Susskind's programs would provide an English teacher with enough linguistic aberrations to fill a semester's worth of analysis.

Nonetheless, the Department of Education has forged ahead, apparently in the belief that ample evidence—to quote Ms. Richards again—"shows that learning increases when information is presented in a dramatic setting, and that television can do this better than any other medium." The most charitable response to this claim is that it is misleading. George Comstock and his associates have reviewed 2,800 studies on the general topic of television's influence on behavior, including cognitive processing, and are unable to point to persuasive evidence that "learning increases when information is presented in a dramatic setting."[2] Indeed, in studies conducted by Cohen and Salomon; Meringoff; Jacoby, Hoyer and Sheluga; Stauffer, Frost and Rybolt; Stern; Wilson; Neuman; Katz, Adoni and Parness; and Gunter, quite the opposite conclusion is justified.[3] Jacoby et al. found, for example, that only 3.5 percent of viewers were able to answer successfully twelve true/false questions concerning two thirty-second segments of commercial television programs and advertisements. Stauffer et al. found in studying students' responses to a news program transmitted via television, radio and print, that print significantly increased correct responses to questions regarding the names of people and numbers contained in the material. Stern reported that 51 percent of viewers could not recall a single item of news a few minutes after viewing a news program on television. Wilson found that the average television viewer could retain only 20 percent of the information contained in a fictional televised news story. Katz et al. found that 21 percent of television viewers could not recall any news items within one hour of broadcast. On the basis of his and other studies, Salomon has concluded that "the meanings secured from television are more likely to be segmented, concrete and less inferential, and those secured from reading have a higher likelihood of being better tied to one's stored knowledge and thus are more likely to be inferential." [4] In other words, so far as many reputable studies are concerned, television viewing does not significantly increase learning, is inferior to and less likely than print to cultivate higher-order, inferential thinking.

But one must not make too much of the rhetoric of grantsmanship. We are all inclined to transform our hopes into tenuous claims when an important project is at stake. Besides, I have no doubt that Ms. Richards can direct us to several studies that lend support to her enthusiasm. The point is that if you want money for the redundant purpose of getting children to watch even more television than they already do—and dramatizations at that—you have to escalate the rhetoric to Herculean proportions.

What is of greatest significance about "The Voyage of the Mimi" is that the content selected was obviously chosen because it is eminently *televisible*. Why are these students studying the behavior of humpback whales? How critical is it that the "academic themes" of navigational and map-reading skills be learned? Navigational skills have never been considered an "academic theme" and in fact seem singularly inappropriate for most students in big cities. Why has it been decided that "whales and their environment" is a subject of such compelling interest that an entire year's work should be given to it?

I would suggest that "The Voyage of the Mimi" was conceived by someone's asking the question, What is television good for?, not, What is education good for? Television is good for dramatizations, shipwrecks, seafaring adventures, crusty old sea captains, and physicists being interviewed by actor-celebrities. And that, of course, is what we have got in "The Voyage of the Mimi." The fact that this adventure sit-com is accompanied by lavishly illustrated books and computer games only underscores that the television presentation controls the curriculum. The books whose pictures the students will scan and the computer games the students will play are dictated by the content of the television shows, not the other way around. Books, it would appear, have now become an audio-visual aid; the principal carrier of the content of education is the television show, and its principal claim for a preeminent place in the curriculum is that it is entertaining. Of course, a television production can be used to stimulate interest in lessons, or even as the focal point of a lesson. But what is happening here is that the content of the school curriculum is being determined by the character of television, and even worse, that character is apparently not included as part of what is studied. One would have thought that the school room is the proper place for students to inquire into the ways in which media of all kinds—including television—shape people's attitudes and perceptions. Since our students will have watched approximately sixteen thousand hours of television by high school's end, questions should have arisen, even in the minds of officials at the Department of Education, about who will teach our students how to look at television, and when not to, and with what critical equipment when they do. "The Voyage of the Mimi" project bypasses these questions; indeed, hopes that the students will immerse themselves in the dramatizations in the same frame of mind used when watching "St. Elsewhere" or "Hill Street Blues." (One may also assume that what is called "computer literacy" does not involve raising questions about the cognitive biases and social effects of the computer, which, I would venture, are the most important questions to address about new technologies.)

"The Voyage of the Mimi," in other words, spent $3.65 million for the purpose of using media in exactly the manner that media merchants want them to be used—mindlessly and invisibly, as if media themselves have no epistemological or political agenda. And, in the end, what will the students have learned? They will, to be sure, have learned something about whales, perhaps about navigation and map reading, most of which they could have learned just as well by other means. Mainly, they will have learned that learning is a form of entertainment or, more precisely, that anything worth learning can take the form of an entertainment, and ought to. And they will not rebel if their English teacher asks them to learn the eight parts of speech through the medium of rock music. Or if their social studies teacher sings to them the facts about the War of 1812. Or if their physics comes to them on cookies and T-shirts. Indeed, they will expect it and thus will be well prepared to receive their politics, their religion, their news and their commerce in the same delightful way.

II.

The Huxleyan Warning

There are two ways by which the spirit of a culture may be shriveled. In the first—the Orwellian—culture becomes a prison. In the second—the Huxleyan—culture becomes a burlesque.

No one needs to be reminded that our world is now marred by many prison-cultures whose structure Orwell described accurately in his parables. If one were to read both *1984* and *Animal Farm*, and then for good measure, Arthur Koestler's *Darkness at Noon*, one would have a fairly precise blueprint of the machinery of thought-control as it currently operates in scores of countries and on millions of people. Of course, Orwell was not the first to teach us about the spiritual devastations of tyranny. What is irreplaceable about his work is his insistence that it makes little difference if our wardens are inspired by right- or left-wing ideologies. The gates of the prison are equally impenetrable, surveillance equally rigorous, icon-worship equally pervasive.

What Huxley teaches is that in the age of advanced technology, spiritual devastation is more likely to come from an enemy with a smiling face than from one whose countenance exudes suspicion and hate. In the Huxleyan prophecy, Big Brother does not watch us, by his choice. We watch him, by ours. There is no need for wardens or gates or Ministries of Truth. When a population becomes distracted by trivia, when cultural life is redefined as a perpetual round of entertainments, when serious public conversation becomes a form of baby-talk, when, in short, a people become an audience and their public business a vaudeville act, then a nation finds itself at risk; culture-death is a clear possibility.

In America, Orwell's prophecies are of small relevance, but Huxley's are well under way toward being realized. For America is engaged in the world's most ambitious experiment to accommodate itself to the technological distractions made possible by the electric plug. This is an experiment that began slowly and modestly in the mid-nineteenth century and has now, in the latter half of the twentieth, reached a perverse maturity in America's consuming love-affair with television. As nowhere else in the world, Americans have moved far and fast in bringing to a close the age of the slow-moving printed word, and have granted to television sovereignty over all of their institutions. By ushering in the Age of Television, America has given the world the clearest available glimpse of the Huxleyan future.

Those who speak about this matter must often raise their voices to a near-hysterical pitch, inviting the charge that they are everything from wimps to public nuisances to Jeremiahs. But they do so because what they want others to see appears benign, when it is not invisible altogether. An Orwellian world is much easier to recognize, and to oppose, than a Huxleyan. Everything in our background has prepared us to know and resist a prison when the gates begin to close around us. We are not likely, for example, to be indifferent to the voices of the Sakharovs and the Timmermans and the Walesas. We take arms against such a sea of troubles, buttressed by the spirit of Milton, Bacon, Voltaire, Goethe and Jefferson. But what if there are no cries of anguish to be heard? Who is prepared to take arms against a sea of amusements? To whom do we complain, and when, and in what tone of voice, when serious discourse dissolves into giggles? What is the antidote to a culture's being drained by laughter?

I fear that our philosophers have given us no guidance in this matter. Their warnings have customarily been directed against those consciously formulated ideologies that appeal to the worst tendencies in human nature. But what is happening in America is not the design of an articulated ideology. No *Mein Kampf* or *Communist Manifesto* announced its coming. It comes as the unintended consequence of a dramatic change in our modes of public conversation. But it is an ideology nonetheless, for it imposes a way of life, a set of relations among people and ideas, about which there has been no consensus, no discussion and no opposition. Only compliance. Public consciousness has not yet assimilated the point that technology is ideology. This, in spite of the fact that before our very eyes technology has altered every aspect of life in America during the past eighty years. For example, it would have been excusable in 1905 for us to be unprepared for the cultural changes the automobile would bring. Who could have suspected then that the automobile would tell us how we were to conduct our social and sexual lives? Would reorient our ideas about what to do with our forests and cities? Would create new ways of expressing our personal identity and social standing?

But it is much later in the game now, and ignorance of the score is inexcusable. To be unaware that a technology comes equipped with a program for social change, to maintain that technology is neutral, to make the assumption that technology is always a friend to culture is, at this late hour, stupidity plain and simple. Moreover, we have seen enough by now to know that technological changes in our modes of communication are even more ideology-laden than changes in our modes of transportation. Introduce the alphabet to a culture and you change its cognitive habits, its social relations, its notions of community, history and religion. Introduce the printing press with movable type, and you do the same. Introduce speed-of-light transmission of images and you make a cultural revolution. Without a vote. Without polemics. Without guerrilla resistance. Here is ideology, pure if not serene. Here is ideology without words, and all the more powerful for their absence. All that is required to make it stick is a population that devoutly believes in the inevitability of progress. And in this sense, all Americans are Marxists, for we believe nothing if not that history is moving us toward some preordained paradise and that technology is the force behind that movement.

Thus, there are near insurmountable difficulties for anyone who has written such a book as this, and who wishes to end it with some remedies for the affliction. In the first place, not everyone believes a cure is needed, and in the second, there probably isn't any. But as a true-blue American who has imbibed the unshakable belief that where there is a problem, there must be a solution, I shall conclude with the following suggestions.

We must, as a start, not delude ourselves with preposterous notions such as the straight Luddite position as outlined, for example, in Jerry Mander's *Four Arguments for the Elimination of Television*. Americans will not shut down any part of their technological apparatus, and to suggest that they do so is to make no suggestion at all. It is almost equally unrealistic to expect that nontrivial modifications in the availability of media will ever be made. Many civilized nations limit by law the amount of hours television may operate and thereby mitigate the role television plays in public life. But I believe that this is not a possibility in America. Once having opened the Happy Medium to full public view, we are not likely to countenance even its partial closing. Still, some Americans have been thinking along these lines. As I write, a story appears in *The New York Times* (September 27, 1984) about the plans of the Farmington, Connecticut, Library Council to sponsor a "TV Turnoff." It appears that such an effort was made the previous year, the idea being to get people to stop watching television for one month. The *Times* reports that the turnoff the previous January was widely noted by the media. Ms. Ellen Babcock, whose family participated, is quoted as saying, "It will be interesting to see if the impact is the same this year as last year, when we had terrific media coverage." In other words, Ms. Babcock hopes that by watching television, people will learn that they ought to stop watching television. It is hard to imagine that Ms. Babcock does not see the irony in this position. It is an irony that I have confronted many times in being told that I must appear on television to promote a book that warns people against television. Such are the contradictions of a television-based culture.

In any case, of how much help is a one-month turnoff? It is a mere pittance; that is to say, a penance. How comforting it must be when the folks in Farmington are done with their punishment and can return to their true occupation. Nonetheless, one applauds their effort, as one must applaud the efforts of those who see some relief in limiting certain kinds of content on television—for example, excessive violence, commercials on children's shows, etc. I am particularly fond of John Lindsay's suggestion that political commercials be banned from television as we now ban cigarette and liquor commercials. I would gladly testify before the Federal Communications Commission as to the manifold merits of this excellent idea. To those who would oppose my testimony by claiming that such a ban is a clear violation of the First Amendment, I would offer a compromise: Require all political commercials to be preceded by a short statement to the effect that common sense has determined that watching political commercials is hazardous to the intellectual health of the community.

I am not very optimistic about anyone's taking this suggestion seriously. Neither do I put much stock in proposals to improve the quality of television programs. Television, as I have implied earlier, serves us most usefully when presenting junk-entertainment; it serves us most ill when it co-opts serious modes of discourse—news, politics, science, education, commerce, religion—and turns them into entertainment packages. We would all be better off if television got worse, not better.

"The A-Team" and "Cheers" are no threat to our public health. "60 Minutes," "Eye-Witness News" and "Sesame Street" are.

The problem, in any case, does not reside in *what* people watch. The problem is in *that* we watch. The solution must be found in *how* we watch. For I believe it may fairly be said that we have yet to learn what television is. And the reason is that there has been no worthwhile discussion, let alone widespread public understanding, of what information is and how it gives direction to a culture. There is a certain poignancy in this, since there are no people who more frequently and enthusiastically use such phrases as "the information age," "the information explosion," and "the information society." We have apparently advanced to the point where we have grasped the idea that a change in the forms, volume, speed and context of information *means* something, but we have not got any further.

What is information? Or more precisely, what *are* information? What are its various forms? What conceptions of intelligence, wisdom and learning does each form insist upon? What conceptions does each form neglect or mock? What are the main psychic effects of each form? What is the relation between information and reason? What is the kind of information that best facilitates thinking? Is there a moral bias to each information form? What does it mean to say that there is too much information? How would one know? What redefinitions of important cultural meanings do new sources, speeds, contexts and forms of information require? Does television, for example, give a new meaning to "piety," to "patriotism," to "privacy"? Does television give a new meaning to "judgment" or to "understanding"? How do different forms of information persuade? Is a newspaper's "public" different from television's "public"? How do different information forms dictate the type of content that is expressed?

These questions, and dozens more like them, are the means through which it might be possible for Americans to begin talking back to their television sets, to use Nicholas Johnson's phrase. For no medium is excessively dangerous if its users understand what its dangers are. It is not important that those who ask the questions arrive at my answers or Marshall McLuhan's (quite different answers, by the way). This is an instance in which the asking of the questions is sufficient. To ask is to break the spell. To which I might add that questions about the psychic, political and social effects of information are as applicable to the computer as to television. Although I believe the computer to be a vastly overrated technology, I mention it here because, clearly, Americans have accorded it their customary mindless inattention; which means they will use it as they are told, without a whimper. Thus, a central thesis of computer technology—that the principal difficulty we have in solving problems stems from insufficient data—will go unexamined. Until, years from now, when it will be noticed that the massive collection and speed-of-light retrieval of data have been of great value to large-scale organizations but have solved very little of importance to most people and have created at least as many problems for them as they may have solved.

In any case, the point I am trying to make is that only through a deep and unfailing awareness of the structure and effects of information, through a demystification of media, is there any hope of our gaining some measure of control over television, or the computer, or any other medium. How is such media consciousness to be achieved? There are only two answers that come to mind, one of which is nonsense and can be dismissed almost at once; the other is desperate but it is all we have.

The nonsensical answer is to create television programs whose intent would be, not to get people to stop watching television but to demonstrate how television ought to be viewed, to show how television recreates and degrades our conception of news, political debate, religious thought, etc. I imagine such demonstrations would of necessity take the form of parodies, along the lines of "Saturday Night Live" and "Monty Python," the idea being to induce a nationwide horse laugh over television's control of public discourse. But, naturally, television would have the last laugh. In order to command an audience large enough to make a difference, one would have to make the programs vastly amusing, in the television style. Thus, the act of criticism itself would, in the end, be co-opted by television. The parodists would become celebrities, would star in movies, and would end up making television commercials.

The desperate answer is to rely on the only mass medium of communication that, in theory, is capable of addressing the problem: our schools. This is the conventional American solution to all dangerous social problems, and is, of course, based on a naive and mystical faith in the efficacy of education. The process rarely works. In the matter at hand, there is even less reason than usual to expect it to. Our schools have not yet even got around to examining the role of the printed word in shaping our culture. Indeed, you will not find two high school seniors in a hundred who could tell you—within a five-hundred-year margin of error—when the alphabet was invented. I suspect most do not even know that the alphabet *was* invented. I have found that when the question is put to them, they appear puzzled, as if one had asked, When were trees invented, or clouds? It is the very principle of myth, as Roland Barthes pointed out, that it transforms history into nature, and to ask of our schools that they engage in the task of de-mythologizing media is to ask something the schools have never done.

And yet there is reason to suppose that the situation is not hopeless. Educators are not unaware of the effects of television on their students. Stimulated by the arrival of the computer, they discuss it a great deal—which is to say, they have become somewhat "media conscious." It is true enough that much of their consciousness centers on the question, How can we use television (or the computer, or word processor) to control education? They have not yet got to the question, How can we use education to control television (or the computer, or word processor)? But our reach for solutions ought to exceed our present grasp, or what's our dreaming for? Besides, it is an acknowledged task of the schools to assist the young in learning how to interpret the symbols of their culture. That this task should now require that they learn how to distance themselves from their forms of information is not so bizarre an enterprise that we cannot hope for its inclusion in the curriculum; even hope that it will be placed at the center of education.

What I suggest here as a solution is what Aldous Huxley suggested, as well. And I can do no better than he. He believed with H. G. Wells that we are in a race between education and disaster, and he wrote continuously about the necessity of our understanding the politics and epistemology of media. For in the end, he was trying to tell us that what afflicted the people in *Brave New World* was not that they were laughing instead of thinking, but that they did not know what they were laughing about and why they had stopped thinking.

Notes

Chapter 1: The Medium Is the Metaphor

1. As quoted in the *Wisconsin State Journal*, August 24, 1983, Section 3, page 1.
2. Cassirer, p. 43.
3. Frye, p. 227.

Chapter 2: Media as Epistemology

1. Frye, p. 217.
2. Frye, p. 218.
3. Frye, p. 218.
4. As quoted in Ong, "Literacy and the Future of Print," pp. 201–202.
5. Ong, *Orality*, p. 35.
6. Ong, *Orality*, p. 109.
7. Jerome Bruner, in *Studies in Cognitive Growth*, states that growth is "as much from the outside in as from the inside out," and that "much of [cognitive growth] consists in a human being's becoming linked with culturally transmitted 'amplifiers' of motoric, sensory, and reflective capacities." (pp. 1–2)

   According to Goody, in *The Domestication of the Savage Mind*, "[writing] changes the nature of the representations of the world (cognitive processes) for those who cannot [read]." He continues: "The existence of the alphabet therefore changes the type of data that an individual is dealing with, and it changes the repertoire of programmes he has available for treating his data." (p. 110)

   Julian Jaynes, in *The Origins of Consciousness in the Breakdown of the Bicameral Mind,* states that the role of "writing in the break-down of the bicameral voices is tremendously important." He claims that the written word served as a "replacement" for the hallucinogenic image, and took up the right hemispheric function of sorting out and fitting together data.

Walter Ong, in *The Presence of the Word,* and Marshall McLuhan, in *Understanding Media,* stress media's effects on the variations in the ratio and balance among the senses. One might add that as early as 1938, Alfred North Whitehead (in *Modes of Thought*) called attention to the need for a thorough study of the effects of changes in media on the organization of the sensorium.

Chapter 3: Typographic America

1. Franklin, p. 175.
2. Hart, p. 8.
3. Hart, p. 8.
4. Hart, p. 8.
5. Hart, p. 15.
6. Lockridge, p. 184.
7. Lockridge, p. 184.
8. Hart, p. 47.
9. Mumford, p. 136.
10. Stone, p. 42.
11. Hart, p. 31.
12. Boorstin, p. 315.
13. Boorstin, p. 315.
14. Hart, p. 39.
15. Hart, p. 45.
16. Fast, p. x (in Introduction).
17. This press was not the first established on the American continent. The Spanish had established a printing office in Mexico a hundred years earlier.
18. Mott, p. 7.
19. Boorstin, p. 320.
20. Mott, p. 9.
21. Lee, p. 10.

22. Boorstin, p. 326.
23. Boorstin, p. 327.
24. Hart, p. 27.
25. Tocqueville, p. 58.
26. Tocqueville, pp. 5–6.
27. Hart, p. 86.
28. Curti, pp. 353–354.
29. Hart, p. 153.
30. Hart, p. 74.
31. Curti, p. 337.
32. Hart, p. 102.
33. Berger, p. 183.
34. Curti, p. 356.
35. Berger, p. 158.
36. Berger, p. 158.
37. Berger, p. 158.
38. Curti, p. 356.
39. Twain, p. 161.
40. Hofstadter, p. 145.
41. Hofstadter, p. 19.
42. Tocqueville, p. 260.
43. Miller, p. 269.
44. Miller, p. 271.
45. Marx, p. 150.

Chapter 4: The Typographic Mind

1. Sparks, p. 4.
2. Sparks, p. 11.
3. Sparks, p. 87.
4. Questions were continuously raised about the accuracy of the transcriptions of these debates. Robert Hitt was the verbatim reporter for the debates, and he was accused of repairing Lincoln's "illiteracies." The accusations were made, of course, by Lincoln's political enemies, who, perhaps, were dismayed by the impression Lincoln's performances were making on the country. Hitt emphatically denied he had "doctored" any of Lincoln's speeches.

5. Hudson, p. 5.

6. Sparks, p. 86.

7. Mill, p. 64.

8. Hudson, p. 110.

9. Paine, p. 6.

10. Hudson, p. 132.

11. Perry Miller, p. 15.

12. Hudson, p. 65.

13. Hudson, p. 143.

14. Perry Miller, p. 119.

15. Perry Miller, p. 140.

16. Perry Miller, pp. 140–141.

17. Perry Miller, p. 120.

18. Perry Miller, p. 153.

19. Presbrey, p. 244.

20. Presbrey, p. 126.

21. Presbrey, p. 157.

22. Presbrey, p. 235.

23. Anderson, p. 17. In this connection, it is worth citing a letter, dated January 15, 1787, written by Thomas Jefferson to Monsieur de Crève-coeur. In his letter, Jefferson complained that the English were trying to claim credit for an American invention: making the circumference of a wheel out of one single piece of wood. Jefferson speculated that Jersey farmers learned how to do this from their reading of Homer, who described the process clearly. The English must have copied the procedure from Americans, Jefferson wrote, ''because ours are the only farmers who can read Homer.''

Chapter 5: The Peek-a-Boo World

1. Thoreau, p. 36.

2. Harlow, p. 100.

3. Czitrom, pp. 15–16.

4. Sontag, p. 165.

5. Newhall, p. 33.

6. Salomon, p. 36.

7. Sontag, p. 20.
8. Sontag, p. 20.

Chapter 6: *The Age of Show Business*

1. On July 20, 1984, *The New York Times* reported that the Chinese National Television network had contracted with CBS to broadcast sixty-four hours of CBS programming in China. Contracts with NBC and ABC are sure to follow. One hopes that the Chinese understand that such transactions are of great political consequence. The Gang of Four is as nothing compared with the Gang of Three.
2. This story was carried by several newspapers, including the *Wisconsin State Journal,* February 24, 1983, Section 4, p. 2.
3. As quoted in *The New York Times,* June 7, 1984, Section A, p. 20.

Chapter 7: "Now . . . This"

1. For a fairly thorough report on Ms. Craft's suit, see *The New York Times,* July 29, 1983.
2. MacNeil, p. 2.
3. MacNeil, p. 4.
4. See *Time,* July 9, 1984, p. 69.

Chapter 8: *Shuffle Off to Bethlehem*

1. Graham, pp. 5–8. For a detailed analysis of Graham's style, see Michael Real's *Mass Mediated Culture.* For an amusing and vitriolic one, see Roland Barthes' "Billy Graham at the Winter Cyclodome," in *The Eiffel Tower and Other Mythologies.* Barthes says, "If God really does speak through the mouth of Dr. Graham, then God is a real blockhead."
2. As quoted in "Religion in Broadcasting," by Robert Abelman and Kimberly Neuendorf, p. 2. This study was funded by a grant from Unda-USA, Washington, D.C.
3. Armstrong, p. 137.
4. Arendt, p. 352.

Chapter 9: Reach Out and Elect Someone

1. Drew, p. 263.
2. Moran, p. 122.
3. Rosen, p. 162.
4. Quoted from a speech given on March, 27, 1984, at the Jewish Museum in New York City on the occasion of a conference of the National Jewish Archive of Broadcasting.
5. Moran, p. 125.
6. From a speech given at the twenty-fourth Media Ecology Conference, April 26, 1982, in Saugerties, New York. For a full account of Dean Gerbner's views, see "Television: The New State Religion," *Et cetera* 34:2 (June, 1977): 145–150.

Chapter 10: Teaching as an Amusing Activity

1. Dewey, p. 48.
2. G. Comstock, S. Chaffee, N. Katzman, M. McCombs, and D. Roberts, *Television and Human Behavior* (New York: Columbia University Press, 1978).
3. A. Cohen and G. Salomon, "Children's Literate Television Viewing: Surprises and Possible Explanations," *Journal of Communication* 29 (1979): 156–163; L. M. Meringoff, "What Pictures Can and Can't Do for Children's Story Comprehension," paper presented at the annual meeting of the American Educational Research Association, April, 1982; J. Jacoby, W. D. Hoyer and D. A. Sheluga, *Miscomprehension of Televised Communications* (New York: The Educational Foundation of the American Association of Advertising Agencies, 1980); J. Stauffer, R. Frost and W. Rybolt, "Recall and Learning from Broadcast News: Is Print Better?," *Journal of Broadcasting* (Summer, 1981): 253–262; A. Stern, "A Study for the National Association for Broadcasting," in M. Barret (ed.), *The Politics of Broadcasting, 1971–1972* (New York: Thomas Y. Crowell, 1973); C. E. Wilson, "The Effect of a Medium on Loss of Information," *Journalism Quarterly* 51 (Spring, 1974): 111–115; W. R. Neuman, "Patterns of Recall Among Television News Viewers," *Public Opinion Quarterly* 40 (1976): 118–125; E. Katz, H. Adoni

and P. Parness, "Remembering the News: What the Pictures Add to Recall," *Journalism Quarterly* 54 (1977): 233–242; B. Gunter, "Remembering Television News: Effects of Picture Content," *Journal of General Psychology* 102 (1980): 127–133.

4. Salomon, p. 81.

Bibliography

Anderson, Paul. *Platonism in the Midwest*. Philadelphia: Temple University Publications, 1963.

Arendt, Hannah. "Society and Culture," in *The Human Dialogue*, edited by Floyd Matson and Ashley Montagu. Glencoe, Ill.: Free Press, 1967.

Armstrong, Ben. *The Electric Church*. Nashville: Thomas Nelson, 1979.

Berger, Max. *The British Traveler in America, 1836–1860*. New York: Columbia University Press, 1943.

Boorstin, Daniel J. *The Americans: The Colonial Experience*. New York: Vintage Books, 1958.

Cassirer, Ernst. *An Essay on Man*. Garden City, N.Y.: Doubleday Anchor, 1956.

Curti, Merle. *The Growth of American Thought*. New York: Harper & Row, 1951.

Czitrom, Daniel. *Media and the American Mind: From Morse to McLuhan*. Chapel Hill: University of North Carolina Press, 1982.

Dewey, John. *Experience and Education*. The Kappa Delta Pi Lectures. London: Collier Books, 1963.

Drew, Elizabeth. *Portrait of an Election: The 1980 Presidential Campaign*. New York: Simon and Schuster, 1981.

Eisenstein, Elizabeth. *The Printing Press as an Agent of Change*. New York: Cambridge University Press, 1979.

Fast, Howard. Introduction to *Rights of Man,* by Thomas Paine. New York: Heritage Press, 1961.

Franklin, Benjamin. *The Autobiography of Benjamin Franklin*. New York: Magnum Books, 1968.

Frye, Northrop. *The Great Code: The Bible and Literature*. Toronto: Academic Press, 1981.

Graham, Billy. "The Future of TV Evangelism." *TV Guide* 31:10 (1983).

Harlow, Alvin Fay. *Old Wires and New Waves: The History of the Telegraph, Telephone and Wireless.* New York: Appleton-Century, 1936.

Hart, James D. *The Popular Book: A History of America's Literary Taste.* New York: Oxford University Press, 1950.

Hofstadter, Richard. *Anti-Intellectualism in American Life.* New York: Alfred A. Knopf, 1964.

Hudson, Winthrop. *Religion in America.* New York: Charles Scribner's Sons, 1965.

Lee, James Melvin. *History of American Journalism.* Boston: Houghton Mifflin, 1917.

Lockridge, Kenneth. "Literacy in Early America, 1650–1800," in *Literacy and Social Development in the West: A Reader,* edited by Harvey J. Graff. New York: Cambridge University Press, 1981.

MacNeil, Robert. "Is Television Shortening Our Attention Span?" *New York University Education Quarterly* 14:2 (Winter, 1983).

Marx, Karl, and Friedrich Engels. *The German Ideology.* New York: International Publishers, 1972.

Mill, John Stuart. *Autobiography and Other Writings.* Boston: Houghton Mifflin, 1969.

Miller, John C. *The First Frontier: Life in Colonial America.* New York: Dell, 1966.

Miller, Perry. *The Life of the Mind in America: From the Revolution to the Civil War.* New York: Harcourt, Brace and World, 1965.

Moran, Terence. "Politics 1984: That's Entertainment." *Et cetera* 41:2 (Summer, 1984).

Mott, Frank Luther. *American Journalism: A History of Newspapers in the U.S. through 260 Years, 1690 to 1950.* New York: Macmillan, 1950.

Mumford, Lewis. *Technics and Civilization.* New York: Harcourt, Brace and World, 1934.

Newhall, Beaumont. *The History of Photography from 1839 to the Present Day.* New York: Museum of Modern Art, 1964.

Ong, Walter. "Literacy and the Future of Print." *Journal of Communication* 30:1 (Winter, 1980).

Ong, Walter. *Orality and Literacy.* New York: Methuen, 1982.

Paine, Thomas. *The Age of Reason.* New York: Peter Eckler Publishing Co., 1919.

Presbrey, Frank. *The History and Development of Advertising.* Garden City, N.Y.: Doubleday, Doran and Co., 1929.

Rosen, Jay. "Advertising's Slow Suicide." *Et cetera* 41:2 (Summer, 1984).

Salomon, Gavriel. *Interaction of Media, Cognition and Learning.* San Francisco: Jossey-Bass, 1979.

Sontag, Susan. *On Photography.* New York: Farrar, Straus and Giroux, 1977.

Sparks, Edwin Erle, ed. *The Lincoln-Douglas Debates of 1858.* Vol. I. Springfield, Ill.: Illinois State Historical Library, 1908.

Stone, Lawrence. "The Educational Revolution in England, 1500–1640." *Past and Present* 28 (July, 1964).

Thoreau, Henry David. *Walden.* Riverside Editions. Boston: Houghton Mifflin, 1957.

Tocqueville, Alexis de. *Democracy in America.* New York: Vintage Books, 1954.

Twain, Mark. *The Autobiography of Mark Twain.* New York: Harper and Bros., 1959.

Index